Every dress tells a story

Dreaming of Dior

Charlotte Smith

Illustrated by Grant Cowan

ATRIA BOOKS

New York   London   Toronto   Sydney

ATRIA BOOKS
A Division of Simon & Schuster, Inc.
1230 Avenue of the Americas
New York, NY 10020

Text copyright © 2009 by Charlotte Smith
Illustrations copyright © 2009 by Grant Cowan
Originally published in Australia in 2009 by HarperCollins Publishers Australia Pty Limited

First Atria Books hardcover edition April 2010

ATRIA BOOKS and colophon are trademarks of Simon & Schuster, Inc.

For information about special discounts for bulk purchases, please contact Simon & Schuster Special Sales at 1-866-506-1949 or business@simonandschuster.com.

The Simon & Schuster Speakers Bureau can bring authors to your live event. For more information or to book an event, contact the Simon & Schuster Speakers Bureau at 1-866-248-3049 or visit our website at www.simonspeakers.com.

Designed by Jay Ryves at Future Classic

Manufactured in China

10   9   8   7   6   5   4   3   2   1

Library of Congress Cataloging-in-Publication Data

Smith, Charlotte.
Dreaming of Dior : every dress tells a story / Charlotte Smith ; illustrated by Grant Cowan.—1st ed.
    p. cm.
1. Vintage clothing—Collectors and collecting. 2. Women's clothing—Collectors and collecting. 3. Fashion design—Collectors and collecting. I. Title.

NK4704 .S52 2009
746.9'2074—dc22

2009045026

ISBN 978-1-4391-8755-5
ISBN 978-1-4391-8757-9 (ebook)

For Doris

Inheriting a priceless vintage clothing collection containing more than three thousand pieces sounds like every woman's dream come true.

But all I could think after my American godmother Doris Darnell told me her invaluable legacy was on its way across the world to me was: 'What on earth am I going to do with it?'

Doris's collection had been a lifetime labour of love for her, more precious than any treasure I knew of, and she had chosen me as custodian. I was simply overwhelmed.

That is, until the first box arrived at my home in the Blue Mountains. I peeled back the packing tape, pushed aside layers of white tissue and caught my breath at what lay inside. It was a gown of gossamer silk in the palest cream with silver beads glistening over and beyond the bodice; panels of frothy chiffon slipped through my hands as I raised it to the light. I had unearthed my first treasure. I was instantly enchanted, as Doris knew I would be.

For the next three months Christmas came every day. Out came strapless ballgowns with vast, sumptuous skirts of taffeta and moiré silk, velvet hats bedecked with exotic plumes, organdie party dresses in every style and hue … and every stitch, every sequin, ribbon and silk petal reminded me of Doris.

When I was a child growing up in Philadelphia, Doris was the ultimate fairy godmother. Tall and elegant, flamboyant and utterly charming, she was exotic and unpredictable in a thrilling way. She always dressed in clothes from a time long ago, swishing bustle skirts, lace blouses and trailing feather boas. Clothes that no one else wore, and no one else could wear with quite the sense of drama that Doris did.

I grew up thinking everyone had a special room in their house full of nineteenth-century hats and crocodile handbags, and that every woman had - or should have - wardrobes and trunks filled with rainbows of shimmering gowns.

Each time I visited Doris, the two of us would climb the impossibly narrow and steep staircase to the top floor of her townhouse and lose ourselves for an hour or two amid her latest acquisitions and old favourites. For me this was where magic happened, brought alive by Doris's wonderful stories about the dresses and the women who wore them. Her eyes would sparkle as she recounted the adventures of 1920s flappers, Edwardian ladies at high tea, new brides, debutantes and pioneer women. And it is these stories that make her collection unique.

Doris's collection is a spellbinding journey spanning two hundred and five years, from 1790 to 1995, and encompassing famous couturiers like Lucile, Madeline Vionnet, Dior, Galanos and Jean Muir, but not one bit of it was purchased by her. They are all gifts from friends and acquaintances who either knew or had heard of her legendary 'hobby'. As the Quaker saying goes, every piece was 'given in love and in trust'. Doris was a Quaker her whole life, and while her passion for clothes and accessories was frowned upon as immodest and frivolous by the elders of her religion, her passion remained as irrepressible as her character.

In the spirit of love and trust, Doris devoted the last few decades of her life to sharing her collection with the world. Throughout the 1970s and 1980s, Doris became well known throughout the east coast of the United States and beyond for her 'living fashion' talks, which she would give in museums, college halls and even on cruises around the world, including the *QEII*, donating her speaking fees to the Quaker Society of Friends. Her audiences were invariably so enchanted by her shows that they would donate some of their own treasures to the collection, from a great aunt's pair of Victorian dancing slippers to the latest designer gowns by Chanel and Dior. And so the collection continued to grow, more and more stories were added to share, until the baton was passed on to me.

The treasures that lay before me were worth a fortune. Selling them would set me up for life, but enticing as that thought was, I could never consider such a thing or the idea of them being broken up by donation to museums or other collections. I still had no idea what to do with the collection, but somehow, like Doris, I would find a way to share it, and to keep it growing. Over the years, Doris had loaned me some of these gowns to wear, for a ball in Oxfordshire, a wedding in Monaco ... I had so many stories I could add too.

Then, among the last of Doris's boxes, I found her catalogue notes - the notes of all her stories, of the dresses and the women who wore them. As I pored over Doris's words - her wit, wonder and wisdom - the true value of what I had been bequeathed hit home. This wasn't a mere collection of beautiful things, it was a collection of life. Women's lives. Tiny snapshots of our joys and disappointments, our entrances and exits triumphant and tragic - and sometimes tragically hilarious.

And so, in the spirit of love and trust, I - and the inimitable Doris Darnell - share some of those moments with you now.

Charlotte Smith

Dearest Charlotte,

You cannot imagine how happy I am to learn that you are thrilled to have me pass on to you my collection of clothing and accessories of other eras.

Ever since I was a teenager, I have loved to dress up and I still do! Family and friends and friends of friends heard of the old trunk in my attic where I stored my dress-up clothes and started adding to my collection as they cleared out ancestral attics and wondered what to do with all that stuff. That's when my collection really started to grow!

It's been hard, if not impossible, for me to turn down any gifts, because I soon discovered that I was not just collecting dress-up clothes, but, in addition, each piece was a springboard to history. Each donor told me the story of the woman or man who wore the clothing, fascinating stories of other times, sometimes full of joy, other times grief, sometimes bitterness, other times heartache. In my opinion these stories make my clothing three dimensional and in some odd way the people who wore the clothing come alive again in the telling. I am giving you all the stories so that they can continue to be an extension of each outfit.

You ask me what everything I am giving you is worth if you have to declare a value. I have a hard time with that question. I have never bought a single thing nor has anything been appraised. I am giving you a part of my life. I have been a trusted custodian and I am delighted that you see yourself in that same capacity.

The contents of our home are insured for a modest amount with no mention of my clothing. If our house burned down and we lost everything, all of the stories, the glimpses of history, would have no value without the clothing. Money could not replace what I had lost, so why insure?

If I had to come up with something, I would call my gift to you 'old-fashioned clothing with stories about the people who wore the clothes'. They have been treasured by me, but never evaluated. I had planned to leave everything to you in my will, dear godchild, but I am 87 years of age and feel now is the time. So here it is with my blessing!

Love, love, Doris

E very woman has a dress she can't bear to part with because it holds too many memories. For Doris, it was love at first sight in a shop window - a peach slipper satin ballgown that seemed to glow as if lit from within.

But for a scholarship student in 1936, the price tag of $40 - almost half the cost of her room and board for the year - meant owning it was an impossible dream. Then one day a SALE sign appeared and Doris found a way.

Her dream dress made its debut at her first college dance in 1936, escorted by a handsome Rutgers University student, Howard Darnell. Tall, blond and an excellent dancer, Howard was whisked away all too soon, thanks to a Bryn Mawr tradition allowing classmates to claim others' dance partners.

Glowing in her new dress, Doris herself was claimed by the handsome Mel Ferrer, later to become a screen idol and Audrey Hepburn's husband. She was floating on air until she found Howard later: 'He was rigid with anger. When I asked him what on earth was wrong, he replied: "I came to dance with you and not a roomful of strangers!"

Three months later they were engaged.

Classic, chic, elegant. It's pure 1960s glamor. Rich black crepe de chine to ankle and wrist, this evening gown is ingeniously constructed to gently caress each curve of a woman's body, giving me the perfect silhouette. So I like to think.

Above its sleek off-the-shoulder bodice, sheer silk rises to a sumptuous collar of marabou feathers encircling the neck. Another circlet of feathers floats at the base of each sleeve. Outrageously lavish and yet subtle.

It would be a sin to add a single thing to adorn it. I just scoop up my hair and wear a pair of diamond stud earrings. Choose a simple black evening bag that will disappear against the fabric, stilettos with finely pointed toes, and my favourite oriental scent.

It fits me like a glove - and so it should, since my own very special fairy godmother left it to me.

One of only two precious evening dresses my godmother Doris could afford during her college years, this drop-dead elegant 1930s gown shows her inimitable style.

But its daring low back, all the rage at the time, upset Doris's mother, Faith. She observed wryly: 'Doris's impression is that one tended to take off for the dance wearing the jacket and reassuring one's parents about being well covered, and then take the jacket off as soon as you arrived so that you were viewed in all your glory.'

It's hard to imagine this demure 1920s dress causing a scandal, but there was a time when a glimpse of stocking was looked on as something shocking. After it was modelled at one of Doris's shows, one man told her it bought back fond memories of seeing his first 'really short' dress in San Francisco at the tender age of ten.

Sent off to town on an errand, young Tom was stopped in his tracks by the sight of a beautiful young woman in the shortest dress he had ever seen. When she paused at the trolley stop it suddenly dawned on him that in order to get up into the trolley this vision of loveliness might have to reveal even more of a glimpse of her legs. Crossing the street for a better view, he saw he wasn't alone. A group of grown men had gathered outside a store for the same reason.

Much to the delight of her audience, as the lady in question stepped up to the trolley she discovered her dress was a little too snug and she had to pull it up a tad higher to get in. The sight was too much for the owner of the store, who exclaimed 'Jesus Christ!' as the trolley chugged off. Tom remembered thinking 'Amen to that!'

Made for misbehaving, this 1960s cobalt-blue chiffon cocktail dress with a sequinned collar was the perfect choice for the guest of honour at a glamorous party to mark a landmark birthday.

The celebration went into the wee hours and beyond, helped along by a glittering circle of friends, including Princess Grace of Monaco, and plenty of French champagne. But with a dress like this and a few little birthday jewels from Cartier, the birthday girl was assured centre stage.

After all, it's not every day a gal gets to celebrate turning eighty.

Designed by the famous Lucile, this gown was worn by Quaker Elizabeth Vaughn in 1911 when she wed Edwin Williams, her second husband. Elizabeth obviously had no truck with the Quaker belief of dressing simply.

Lucile, also known as Lady Duff Gordon, began dressmaking in the late 1800s to support her daughter after a short-lived first marriage. Her empire grew to include boutiques in London, New York, Paris and Chicago to meet the demand for her 'Gowns of Emotion'. A former lingerie designer, Lucile created dresses that were unashamedly romantic, adorned with delicate pastel-coloured ribbons and flowers.

Lucile was one of the first designers to license her name for perfumes, brassieres and even luxury car interiors. She also created a cheaper fashion line for a chain store, Sears Roebuck & Co.

In 1912 Lucile and her husband survived the sinking of the *Titanic* by climbing into the first lifeboat. But as each lifeboat could carry forty people and there were only twelve on board when they were rescued, the Duff Gordons were taken to court by the Board of Transport. While they were found not guilty of hindering the rescue of others, some say the scandal ended Lucile's popularity.

This cheeky little 1970s mini has had more than a few adventures in its time but this is my favourite from the daughter of its original owner …

'My mother told me a friend of hers borrowed this dress for a date. She arrived home late to find her mother in the kitchen in her dressing gown. After having a cup of tea and an innocent chat, she said goodnight and sighed with relief as she went to bed. She was sure her mother had no idea she had been drinking rum down by the river with her boyfriend. Then she looked in the mirror and realised her dress was on inside out. Her mother never said a thing.

'I asked my mother recently if it was really "a friend" this happened to. She looked a little embarrassed and said "No, it was me. But that was the night I met your father".'

This Ungaro sunflower dress demands attention - and you have to expect consequences if you dare to wear it. I wore it to a 1992 dinner at Spago's in Hollywood, then the place everyone went to see and be seen. I went with two screenwriter friends to celebrate in style after they sold a script.

Any second thoughts I'd had about my bold wardrobe choice magically disappeared after we were seated in prime position right next to Michelle Pfeiffer's table. The champagne flowed and I was on top of the world. That was until I woke up the next morning, still in my dress, and started to remember just what else I had dared to do last night.

I blame the dress ...

T wenty-year-old Peggy Marvel loved nothing better
than buying a new dress - until she met Eugene Quigg,
whom she loved even more.

Always exquisitely dressed, Peggy embraced haute couture
from an early age. Determined his daughter would fit in at
an exclusive new school, her father sent her to be outfitted
in Paris - and from her first Dior piece she was smitten.

As soon as they married, Eugene set out to spoil his wife as
only a man in love - who also happened to be exceptionally
wealthy - could. Eugene encouraged Peggy to buy any
designer dress her heart desired, even hiring a personal
buyer to help her hunt out the latest fashions in New York,
London and Paris.

Peggy's favourite ritual was unveiling each new piece to her
husband. Every night she would dress carefully for dinner
and sweep down the curving staircase of their stately
Richmond home to Eugene, who would be waiting with
a kiss as his seal of approval.

Hand embroidered with sequins and glass beads in Hong
Kong, this 1960s sheath dress and jacket was the last outfit
Peggy modelled for Eugene before he died. Heartbroken,
she never wore it again.

It was 1934 and Doris's first Halloween party at her new high school. It was a costume party so she asked her mother to find her something special in her 'dress-up' trunk.

Thanks to her choice, an otherworldly black taffeta gown with a long train, Doris did feel special. Most of the partygoers went the usual route and came as ghosts, wearing a torn sheet made into a 'peculiar and lumpy arrangement', as she recalls. But newcomer Doris was a standout and thoroughly enjoyed all the attention, especially from the boys.

When the party was over and the students were walking up the stairs, someone stepped on Doris's train and ripped it. Her heart sank - her mother expected her to take care of her things and she would be disappointed.

Two days later she received a note in the mail: 'I am the clod who stepped on your train and I would like to get to know you better'. It was signed 'Howard Darnell'.

Doris and Howard went out on their first date soon after.

B old and beautiful, this 1970s orange dress with a jewelled belt was a perfect match for a stylish jetsetter who was always on the lookout for little treasures for Doris's collection or something unique her friend might like showing off. One day Marai found the perfect gift, according to Doris:

'Since I need to wear glasses to read the menu in a restaurant and dislike pulling out my sensible bifocals, she got me a gold lorgnette, which I can fold and put into my handbag and pull out to read the menu with great style and then tuck it away again. I don't feel as though I'm wearing glasses, which instantly shifts my feeling as to who I am from a carefree, wished-she-were-dramatic kind of woman to a sensible and practical one. And "sensible" is a word I never want to be called.'

This electric blue satin gown was just one of the many show-stopping designer outfits owned by concert pianist Gordy Wallace in the 1980s.

Gordy had two grand pianos in her home and twice a year she would throw enormous parties and invite all sorts of interesting people, much to the delight of Doris. Her pianos were the focus of her parties with either her playing or her friends giving an impromptu concert. Seemingly endless supplies of champagne and caviar kept the guests entertained in any case.

Not only was this grand spectacle Gordy's favourite way of entertaining but she told Doris it was a dandy way of meeting all her social obligations for the year.

Much as she loved Doris and beautiful dresses, Gordy was never interested in wearing anything from her friend's collection and made no bones about the fact she considered vintage nothing more than dusty old clothes. But as she never kept anything - just a select wardrobe of the latest designer clothes - she was as generous as ever in donating many of her best pieces to Doris.

Every woman has to have a little black dress in her survival kit. But when Doris was arming me for a year in Paris with a suitcase full of vintage clothes, she outdid herself with a sensational black raw silk 1960s Dior. So simple yet so, so elegant, this little gem seemed to give me entrée to any soiree.

And no matter where or why I wore it, good things always happened to me in this dress ...

Young Miss Felicity Buxton won more than a few hearts when she wore this sensational pink and black beaded sheath to a dinner dance in 1915.

It was love at first sight for tall, dark and mysterious Owen Thomson, who managed to dance only briefly with Felicity. Sadly, Owen's only distinguishing features during that brief window of opportunity were two left feet and an apparent inability to speak. It would take him months to confess that his lack of conversation was caused by a dreadful attack of the love bug, by which time Felicity was equally smitten.

They were engaged in March 1916, but Owen answered the call of Uncle Sam soon after. Blessedly, he returned from the war, with his two left feet intact, and they were married soon after.

In his letters home, author Henry James talked about meeting a charming young American, Lizzie Boott, in Florence in 1850.

Having showed artistic talent at an early age, Lizzie's father encouraged her to pursue her studies in Paris. There, under the guidance of artist Frank Duveneck, her gift began to flourish. Lizzie and Frank also fell madly in love.

But when Frank asked for Lizzie's hand, her father was horrified. An upstart painter from Cincinnati, no matter how talented, was no match for a daughter of one of Boston's best families. Even though it would be ten years before Frank and Lizzie met again, their feelings never changed. But neither did her father's.

Finally, Frank wrote to Lizzie: 'This is the last time I am going to ask you to marry me. If you say "yes", get on a train, don't tell your father, come to Paris and we will be married.' This time she did not hesitate.

Lizzie and Frank reconciled with Francis Boott, naming their newborn son after him. Sadly, however, just three months later Lizzie died of pneumonia. At her father's request, Frank created a hauntingly beautiful sculpture of Lizzie for her grave in Florence's Allori Cemetary.

This outfit always makes me think of a story Doris told in a lovely gossipy letter she sent to my mother in Hong Kong four days after I was born:

'As I write, I think of last night. When I got home from work last night I looked in the mirror and decided I couldn't go to the Russell Joneses for dinner with the ragged-tag end of a permanent. So I put my bangs on curlers and rolled the hair beside my face and sat on the Davenport with the hairdryer blasting me. When Howard got home he took one look and said he wasn't sure he would have married me if he'd known I could look like that. I pointed out that I was the same person inside and he agreed this was probably true, but the overall effect was not enticing. The end was worth it, I might add. I strongly disapprove of females with their hair in curlers wandering around the house, but I considered this an emergency.'

Emily Price looked positively luminous in a bright purple silk ballgown as her escort swept her onto the dance floor at the Elks Country Club in Savannah in 1951. Clearly delighted to be squiring the woman every man in the room was admiring, he told Emily she was 'a vision in amethyst' and that in medieval times soldiers carried amethyst into battle because it was thought to have magical powers of protection. When he asked Emily if she would be his lucky charm, she smiled serenely, fervently wishing he would go and dance with a more willing partner so that she could talk with a handsome law graduate, Clay R. Thompson, who had caught her eye.

As it turned out, her date had a few too many glasses of Madeira and needed to be escorted home by one of the older gentlemen. Emily didn't mind because Clay gallantly offered to drive her home. It was snowing heavily, and when they pulled up at the kerb in front of her house, he gave her his tuxedo jacket to protect her dress before helping her out of his car. As he escorted her up the path to her doorstep, some snowflakes settled on her skirt, glittering in the lamplight like diamonds, but she was too mesmerised by Clay to worry about saving her dress from ruin.

'Attention must be paid,' says Linda Loman in Arthur Miller's play, *Death of a Salesman*. And that sentiment certainly applied to the owner of this 1950s lace cocktail dress for her electrifying performance as Linda in the 50th anniversary production of the play on Broadway in 1999. Elizabeth Franz garnered the best reviews of her career and picked up her first Tony Award. After years working in repertory theatres across the United States, playing roles in soap operas and small parts in film, she had finally arrived.

Doris witnessed the award-winning performance and said Elizabeth was 'magnificent', as always. For her part, Elizabeth wryly observed that her drama teacher's prediction all those years ago that her best work would come later in life had indeed come true.

Best of all was the verdict from Arthur Miller, who declared hers the best interpretation of the part he had ever seen.

Any woman who has ever dreamed about what it would feel like to sashay down a grand staircase with clouds of chiffon elegantly billowing behind her like Audrey Hepburn in *Funny Face* will understand why the owner of this hot pink evening dress just *had* to do it.

It's a girl thing.

In her sinuous blue chiffon dress, Mary Votaugh Williams looked the part of the quintessential 1920s flapper, ready to shimmy and all that jazz. Indeed, she loved nothing better than literally kicking up her heels at all the best parties in Mississippi.

After one riotously good party, Mary ended up in court, all because she came home at 5 am and saw the milkman making his deliveries to the next-door neighbour.

It just so happened that the same milkman was accused of a serious crime that occurred on the other side of town right at the time Mary was tiptoeing up her front steps. Dressed in her best, the glamorous socialite made the front page as she testified on the milkman's behalf as to his whereabouts, and he was acquitted of the charges.

A Mississippi newspaper tartly noted during the trial: 'They are even involving social butterflies in his support group'. But to the milkman, Mary would always be his guardian angel.

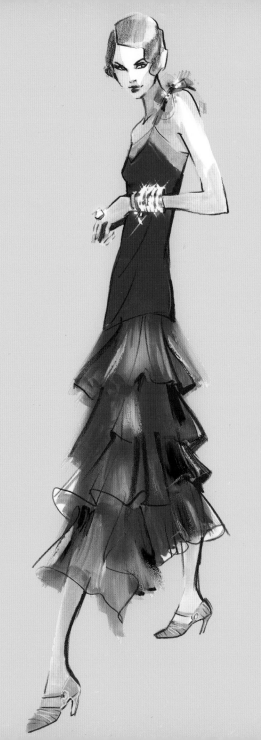

In 1900 it seemed Mrs Edmund Williams spent every other day at yet another lavish tea party where her friends could show off their afternoon-tea gowns of jacquard woven silks, lace, velvet and moiré and hats trimmed with fur or exotic feathers. After all, it was the Belle Epoque - the Beautiful Age - and the wealthy members of society were revelling in it.

But such lavish and ostentatious displays were out of the question for a Quaker like Mrs Williams, who continued to wear her plain brown dresses. She didn't begrudge her friends their fun or disapprove. On the contrary, she loved the opulence and the detail of afternoon-tea gowns. So enchanting did she find them that one day she could not resist commissioning a seamstress to make this breathtaking gown of lime-green silk with striking black velvet trim. Emboldened, she also purchased an enormous hat adorned with an ostrich feather.

Back home, she lovingly hung gown and hat in her armoire. She never wore them, but said the enjoyment they gave her was worth every penny she spent.

Doris's friend Marion always looked as glamorous as any movie star and seemed to own the same endless array of designer outfits. Her secret was a talent for redesigning secondhand clothes so that they looked like the latest designer originals, and often even better.

Her ensembles were so spectacular that they turned more than a few heads over the years. Marion's favourite encounter though was the day she was sashaying down Fifth Ave in New York wearing a feather hat and an impossibly elegant suit, and a presumptuous young man called out: 'Hello, Miss Bergdorf Goodman!'.

There's no doubt Marion looked like she shopped at that prestigious establishment. However, when the bold young man got past her and saw that she wasn't the smashing young woman in her early twenties he had expected but a much more mature grande dame, he immediately apologised profusely. But Marion was delighted.

D oris always thought of this as her *My Fair Lady* cloak because it was every bit as dramatic as the one Eliza, portrayed so unforgettably by Audrey Hepburn, was draped in before her triumph at the ball.

It was worn in the 1930s to the opera, ballet and orchestra recitals by a young woman who never missed an opening night. When her mother died, Emma's father asked her to give up her job teaching to keep house and take care of him. Fortunately her father loved music and ballet as much as his daughter did, so she was constantly going out to opening nights - and dressing the part.

Doris said she knew Emma's job had been important to her, but believed she enjoyed this period of her life even more. In her later years she started to lose her hearing, so Doris was glad Emma had all those years of beautiful music.

As my newly appointed godmother, Doris was bitterly disappointed she couldn't come to visit my mother and me after I entered the world. But Matilda Hospital on The Peak in Hong Kong was a long way from Philadelphia.

As a consolation present, my mother went to her favourite shop in Kowloon and bought this sumptuous beaded and sequined top for Doris.

Doris was over the moon. When the precious package arrived she tried the top on with every skirt in her wardrobe and the collection until she found this perfect match. In a long letter thanking my mother, Doris said she couldn't believe this decadent gift was really for her. She had never owned anything quite so splendid.

In Edwardian times, the proper outfit for ladies pursuing the latest popular outdoor activities like tennis, golf and archery was a cotton day dress decorated lavishly with hand-embroidery.

Archery was a passion for my great uncle, 'Pop', who lived in a gracious Elizabethan manor house called Greenfield, just outside Henley-on-Thames in England. At the turn of the century, Pop and Aunt Sylvia would invite their friends around for a spot of sports and socialising. Pimms was served and the less athletic guests watched the action from under a huge oak tree.

Pop was a great shot, but in the early days of practising his new hobby the household learned to keep a healthy distance. It was a source of some tension between Pop and Aunt Sylvia that he would persist in setting up his targets dangerously close to her glorious rose gardens.

Even when we visited Pop in his late 80s he was still passionate about his archery and determined that we should all learn. I remember the sweet scent of the roses as I did my best to keep the bow and arrow steady, and not impale anyone.

The epitome of 1920s va-va-voom, this beaded flapper dress belongs in a ritzy nightclub where the gin's cold and the piano's hot. So it's not surprising that it was worn by a beautiful and daring young thing who loved to shimmy until the wee hours and whose exploits sometimes made the newspapers.

A leader not a follower, Mary was one of the first in her set to have her hair cut in the latest bob. Her mother-in-law didn't approve of Mary cutting her lovely long auburn hair. But when Mary got appendicitis she announced to her mother-in-law that she simply had to have her hair cut because the length of her hair was draining her strength.

This 1960s gold and mint brocade dress belonged to a friend Doris admired not only for her elegance, but for her compassion and integrity. Dorothy Steere was the person you went to if you were in trouble and she would always tell you the truth. And Doris loved the story of how she became such an honest woman.

When they were little girls, Dorothy and her sister used to love playing in their sprawling backyard until the neighbour's children started to come over and bully them. One day, Dorothy decided she had had enough and told the interlopers she and her sister couldn't play today because they had to go visit their aunt. But as soon as they had escaped indoors, Dorothy felt terrible about telling a lie, the first she had ever told in her life. Her little sister was horrified, which made her feel even more ashamed. Then her mother appeared and said to hurry up and change as their aunt had called to ask them to visit.

Dorothy rushed upstairs and knelt down beside her bed and said: 'Thank you, God, for clearing the air so that the lie I told was not in the end a lie. And I promise I will never tell another lie again'.

In the summer of 1986, a wedding in Monaco led to one of the most unforgettable weeks of my life.

As the bride was the daughter of Prince Rainier of Monaco's right-hand man, it was to be no ordinary wedding. Joining a large group of the groom's friends from New York, I was just thrilled to have the opportunity to see the glamorous backdrop for *To Catch a Thief* for myself, but the prospect of a week of fabulous parties there didn't hurt either.

For the pre-wedding cocktail party, I dressed as only a 24-year-old who felt she had the world at her feet would dare - in a tiny strapless white cocktail dress with stitched silk hot-pink polka dots and a flowing pink scarf. It certainly helped get me the right sort of attention because I met Prince Albert at the bar and we hit it off straight away. He offered to show me around Monte Carlo, and later made good on his promise with a spectacular tour around the Grand Corniche in his silver Porsche.

That was just the opener for what would be a fairytale week.

It was Christmas and I was six. I remember the rustle of her billowing skirt as she led me through the book-lined foyer of her Philadelphia townhouse, past the tree with its twinkling silver baubles and fairy lights. As I followed behind, I was mesmerised by the fur trim on her cloak and her extraordinary hat. I'd never seen anything so grand. She looked like she had stepped out of one of my favourite picture books.

She turned and bent down to show me a basket of holly sprigs and other goodies, and then she smiled at me. My godmother Doris. What she said to me, I don't recall, but from that night on I was smitten.

Every time we went to visit after that I couldn't wait to get inside and see Doris and race up to the third floor where she would lay out her collection of treasures from the past and tell me stories about the women who wore them. For this little girl, it was better than Aladdin's cave.

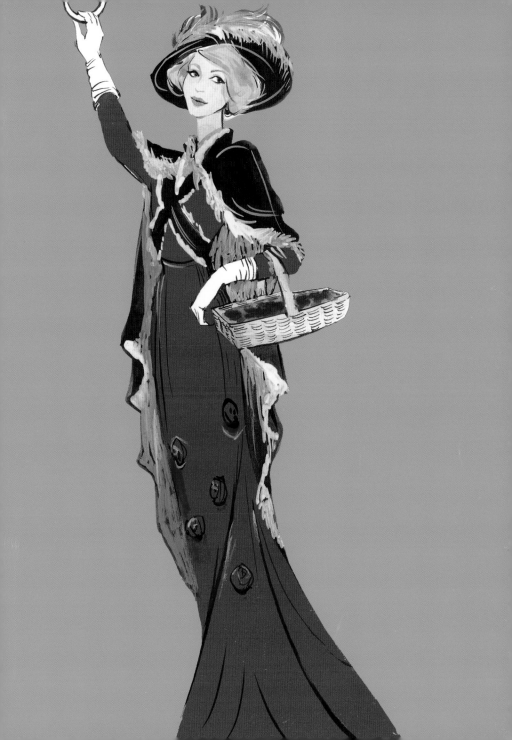

Once again Doris came to my rescue in my hour of need with this spectacular 1950s pink ball gown for a wedding party in Monte Carlo. I needed something out of the ordinary and Doris came through and then some.

The setting overlooking the sea on the terrace of the Hotel de Paris was the last word in romance for a wedding. After the ceremony, our party was invited to enjoy another spectacular view and further celebrations at the clifftop home of the bride's parents. It is here that Prince Albert joined us and the party was complete.

An unforgettable evening …

It's not surprising that on its first outing this sparkling 1950s creation ignited an affair to remember.

A cheeky tomboy who was forever in trouble as a little girl, Alex had caused her parents all sorts of headaches. When caught stealing apples from the next door neighbours, she fell out of their tree and broke her arm. Ever since then the neighbours' older son, Robert, had called her 'Jinx'.

Soon afterwards Alex's parents packed her off to a boarding school in Europe in the desperate hope that she would emerge a lady. As Alex made her grand entrance at a dinner dance ten years later, it seemed all their prayers had been answered.

As soon as Robert saw this vision of loveliness, he strode across the dance floor to cut in and claim her. As her took her in his arms and saw her cheeky smile, he realised that this glamorous stranger was the notorious apple thief.

This bold flowered silk mini by Italian designer Tiziani was made to be the centre of attention. So it's fitting that it was worn with great panache by a woman who had to entertain almost every night as the wife of a diplomat in the 1960s. From postings in Algeria, Paris and Washington, Marty became known as one of those hostesses who always threw a great party and could make anyone feel instantly at ease.

When Marty and her husband retired, she loved visiting Doris because at her house she could happily wear the more glamorous dresses from her extensive wardrobe that would be too 'conspicuous' at neighbourhood gatherings.

One day she brought some outfits to Doris for the collection and agreed to model them so that each one could be photographed for her archives. The trouble was that Marty fell in love all over again with her three-piece Dior suit and had to take it back home. As you would. It *was* Dior, after all.

When I was studying in Paris in the late 1970s, my parents called to let me know that the curator of fashion at the Philadelphia Art Museum, Dus Cavallo, would be in town to set up an exhibition showcasing one of my favourite designers, Elsa Schiaparelli. While he was in Paris he would take me to lunch - I suspect partly to check up on me for my parents and to ensure I had a decent meal.

It was clear I was to be on my best behaviour so I was a little nervous about making a good impression. It was time to pull out something special, a stunning pink knitted mini dress interwoven with tiny sequins I had saved all my hard-earned francs - and gone without croissants for weeks - to own.

As I strode past the Eiffel Tower, I felt confident enough to take on the world - or at least lunch in Paris.

Like many couples who married in the shadow of the First World War, Eleanor Kellogg Chase and Charles Phelps Taft II were determined to make the most of the time they had together. Their 1917 wedding ceremony in Waterbury, Connecticut, was deliberately low-key. Charles wore his military uniform instead of a morning suit, towering lovingly over his petite bride in her delicate silk gown.

Charles was the son of William H. Taft, the 27th president of the United States. In 1917 William was being drawn into controversy over the war in his role as president of the General Conference of Unitarian and other Christian Churches.

But on this day, celebrating the happy union of his son and new daughter-in-law was all that mattered.

An original by French designer Jean Patou, this exquisite 1930s silk dress covered with sequinned flowers was first worn by a beautiful young actress to a performance of her favourite opera, *Madame Butterfly*, in Vienna.

The dress enjoyed a new lease of life in the 1980s when Doris inherited it for her collection. Doris loved it so much she wore it for many special occasions because it was not only beautiful to look at but heavenly to wear, the silk 'as soft as skin'.

In the 1920s Patou was the last word in elegance and designed for actresses such as Constance Bennett, Mary Pickford and Louise Brooks. He is credited with inventing the first designer label, outlining his pockets with a 'J' and 'P'.

In 1925 he branched out into perfumes, 'Amour-Amour', for brunettes, 'Que Sais-je' for blondes and 'Adieu Sagesse' for redheads. But they were eclipsed by 'the most costly perfume in the world' he unveiled in 1931. Jean Patou's 'Joy' may no longer be the most expensive, but it's still the favourite fragrance of women all over the world.

Perfectly sculpted to capture every luscious curve of a fashionable 1940s figure, this elegant black crepe evening dress with its glittering mother-of-pearl lovebirds would turn heads on any red carpet. But such a glamorous dress often only had an audience of one for its owner, Edith Dewee, who would dress for dinner even if just dining at home alone with her husband.

One night a very proper Quaker couple came to call and when they saw Edith in this dress, looking like she was going out on the town, they beat a hasty retreat. As Edith laughingly confided to Doris later, she knew this couple could never have understood. Their conservative Quaker modesty could not conceive of such an extravagant display for simply dining at home.

But dressing for dinner was not only the norm for her social circle, it was one of her great pleasures in life - as it was for Doris. The only difference is Doris would of course only ever wear vintage.

Couturier to Hollywood stars like Joan Crawford and doyennes of style like the Duchess of Windsor, Hattie Carnegie's multimillion-dollar fashion empire began humbly with a small millinery shop on East 10th Street in New York. Her fame reached its peak with the famous Hattie Carnegie boutique at 42 East 49th Street, the first of its kind, featuring not only her own couture line, but several ready-to-wear lines, alongside high fashion imports - Dior, Chanel, Vionnet, Lanvin, Patou and Schiaparelli - and fur, jewellery, perfume and chocolate.

In creating the ultimate emporium for a lady to spend hours indulging her passion for beautiful clothes, accessories and seductive fragrances, Hattie pioneered the boutique concept store. And it was here that Peggy Marvel, one of the many high-society young ladies who religiously read Hattie's column in *Vogue* about the latest style tips, found this fabulous 1930s gown.

With a streamlined silhouette and flowing train, it had a dangerously low back, and was made of silk in Hattie's signature colour, Carnegie blue, intricately embellished with delicate wisps of glittering metallic thread. Peggy simply had to have it. In it, her secret dream of becoming a siren of the silver screen seemed delectably within reach.

When I was nine years old I used to spend hours on my bed dressing up my Barbie, dreaming that one day I would have as many beautiful clothes to wear as she did.

Like many little girls, I thought Barbie was so beautiful with her impossibly slim legs, delicate arched feet - all the better to slip on her high heels - and long slender neck. And of course everything she wore looked great.

But one of my all-time favourites was her pink sweater with fake fur collar, which I combined with a canny little black skirt. When Doris saw me dressing Barbie in this stunning ensemble on one of my visits, she hustled me upstairs, sat me on her bed and told me she'd be right back.

As I heard her come up the hallway, she told me to close my eyes and hold out my hands for a surprise. When I opened them, there was a beautiful pale pink sweater just like Barbie's. Made of the softest lambswool with a dyed fox fur collar and a diamante-studded buckle, it was the most beautiful thing I had ever seen.

Little did I know that it would become part of a wardrobe even Barbie would envy.

This pale blue bustle dress was worn by Miss Jenny Hartigan in 1885. After teaching Sunday school one day, Jenny discovered she had lost her keys. She was positive she had bought them with her to class, but after turning the schoolroom upside down she had to admit defeat.

The only possibility left was that she had simply forgotten to bring them with her, so she walked all the way home to look for them. Her father found them as soon as she turned around. One of her cheeky pupils had discovered the perfect hiding place - on top of her enormous bustle!

As mother of the bride outfits go, this yellow silk organza dress, with its extravagant lace panels and dramatic full skirt, looks more like something Auntie Mame would wear to host one of her infamous parties.

It originally belonged to Lucia Chase, the founder of the American Ballet Theatre in New York. Lucia was renowned for her vast wardrobe of couture gowns and, as she was constantly going to premieres and parties, she rarely wore the same one more than once or twice. When the time came to retire a dress, she'd send it to her sister Nellie in Cincinnati.

As a devoted wife and mother, Nellie's life might have been a little less glamorous than her sister's but it was every bit as busy and fulfilling. Nevertheless, she loved wearing her sister's hand-me-downs because they were so beautiful. In fact, Nellie loved this dress so much that she wore it to each of her four daughters' weddings in the 1940s.

How ironic that just when I was wearing a dress designed by no less than the Queen's favourite couturier I had an unexpected royal encounter of my own.

It was 1988 in London and I was returning from a dinner wearing an outrageously flamboyant Norman Hartnell black jersey dress with a jaunty ostrich-feather fringe. Feeling oh so sophisticated, I was the living embodiment of Hartnell's catchphrase: 'To me, simplicity is the death of the soul'.

As I entered my flat, I heard voices and the laughter of my flatmate and a female companion floating up the hallway from the kitchen. Popping my head around the corner to say hello, I was momentarily stunned to discover that my flatmate's friend was Diana, Princess of Wales.

I'd taken messages from a Diana who sometimes phoned, but I'd had no idea it was this Diana. Although dressed in a simple T-shirt and jeans, she was still one of the most striking and glamorous women I'd ever seen. But it was her friendliness and warmth that left the most enduring impression on me.

This 1970s beaded dress belonged to a New York editor who became a successful painter. When Gay was asked to paint a large mural for Doris and Howard, they suggested she do it in situ, right there in their dining room. Howard invented a clever pulley system for her to ease the mural down to paint and back up again to dry. That way, Gay could turn up while Howard and Doris were out, spread her paints out on the table, pull the canvas down and get to work.

Often the only way they could tell Gay had been there was a slight whiff of turpentine. That was until a dinner guest left the table one night and Howard saw to his horror that the back of his dinner jacket had been imprinted with all the possible colour nuances of hummingbirds flitting through the jungle from the painting. Thinking quickly, Howard turned up the heat. When their flushed guest took off his jacket, Howard offered to hang it up and then sped downstairs to put his paint remover to the test. He succeeded - so well that neither the guest nor Doris had any idea anything was amiss.

S arah Emlen Moore, or Aunt Sallie, as she was known
to her extended family, was the matriarch of a large
and closeknit clan. In 1870 her beloved husband passed
away and she spent the rest of her life behind a black wall
of mourning dress, rarely venturing beyond the gates of
her Philadelphia residence. Her wardrobe consisted of jet-
beaded silk faille and bombazine dresses, black-fringed
mantels and weeping veils.

Her brothers and sisters, and many nieces and nephews,
all made sure she never wanted for company, and most days
one of them would visit. The warmth in her eyes and her
smile had not been extinguished by her bereavement and
the stern, austere exterior of the dowager she tried to effect
invariably failed.

Having had such a long and happy marriage, Aunt Sallie
also had a time-honoured role in her clan. It was tradition to
bring all prospective in-laws over to dinner at her house, so
she could indicate whether or not she approved before they
committed themselves to the union. Aunt Sallie always gave
her seal of approval with a surreptitious wink at the dining
table when the guest under review was looking the other way.

Teetering along in shoes just a little too large, heels sinking into the grass, I can remember feeling ten feet tall when I was finally able to wear the outfit of my dreams, my mother's brightly flowered turquoise silk coat.

It was without doubt the most flamboyant piece of clothing she owned and ever since I could remember I had coveted it, sneaking it out of her cupboard when nobody was looking and twirling around in front of the mirror, admiring the kaleidoscope of pinks, blues and greens, dreaming of when I would be grown up enough to wear it.

My moment finally came when I was twelve and visiting my English godmother Jill in South Devon. As a special treat, I was allowed to enter the 'Best Dressed Lady and Dog' competition at the local Yealmpton fair. My mother let me borrow her colourful silk coat and my godmother let me borrow her sheepdog, Pirate.

There was no doubt in my mind that Pirate and I would win the day.

Southern belles like the one who wore this crinoline in 1860 may have been ladies of leisure, but the strict rules of decorum they had to follow must have often made it seem like work.

Digging through some old records of this period, Doris was tickled by some of the rules of 'Civil War Etiquette'.

For example, on introduction, a married lady might offer her hand but a young unmarried lady definitively may not. Ladies must always wear gloves when outdoors, at church or other formal affairs, but were generously permitted to remove them when eating or drinking. And when manoeuvring an enormous crinoline skirt like this one, they must always be 'ladylike'. When sitting down, they should ask for assistance rather than lifting their skirts onto the chair themselves.

But perhaps some rules of good manners should still apply. A lady should never refuse one gentleman and then accept an invitation to dance with another.

As funky and chic today as it was then, this 1960s Pucci dress belonged to one of the children of Japanese-Americans who were rounded up and kept isolated during the Second World War. The Quaker American Friends Service Committee worked hard to find homes for the children, away from the relocation camps, and this is how Marai became part of Doris's extended family.

Marai later taught at a Quaker school on Long Island and worked at the Japanese NGO office of the United Nations, Japan House and the Japan Society until she retired. Then life became even more interesting, according to Doris:

'Her retirement activity which really does tickle me is to travel to Paris, Japan and New York to be the companion for one of the top Kabuki dancers in the world. He happens to be gay, but occasionally he is asked to bring a girl and as Marai dresses so beautifully and is so sophisticated she is an addition to any gathering.'

Ever the fairy godmother, Doris gave me this stunning black and cerise evening dress for my 18th birthday. I felt so sophisticated and grown up when I wore it for the first time to a black-tie ball in the country. The flamenco-style flounces and split skirt made it the perfect dress for dancing. I was having far too much fun doing just that to notice that it had been snowing steadily outside and by the time the ball ended it was too deep to drive all the way home. But a charming stranger came to the rescue and invited the stranded out-of-towners to stay at his farmhouse in the valley nearby.

In the morning when I sneaked out of bed to explore, I discovered that the house was full of paintings I had only ever seen in art books, including what looked like an original portrait of John F. Kennedy.

It turned out that our rescuer was Jamie Wyeth, an artist from a legendary family of artists. His father was Andrew Wyeth, one of the most renowned painters in the United States, and the creator of one of my favourite paintings, 'Christina's World'.

A riot of aqua and white chiffon flowers, this 1960s hat had quite enough to say without adding to the conversation so it was always worn with a simple Chanel-style suit like this one.

And the stylish combination was captured forever in a snapshot the owner's daughter treasures as a perfect memory of her mother striking a pose in her favourite outfit.

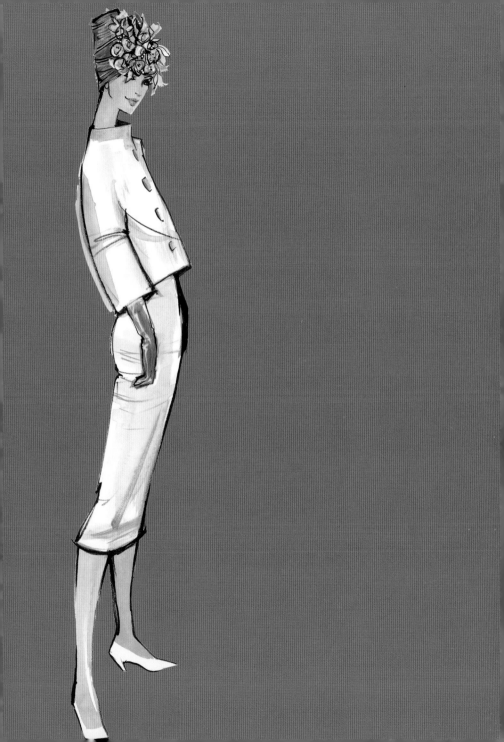

Feathers, rhinestones and sequins floated and shimmered before our eyes as the can-can dancers leapt and kicked in perfect unison across the stage at the Moulin Rouge in Paris.

It was the mid-1980s and I was feeling ever so chic in my sexy Georges Rech black mini, an eight-strand pearl choker and skyscraper stilettos.

The joint was jumping and I remember thinking the essence of what Toulouse-Lautrec captured in his paintings was alive and almost dangerous that night. Perhaps that's what made me want to kick up my heels too, just as generations before me had done in this theatre - or perhaps it was the dress.

Whatever the reason, my yearning to dance must have been written all over my face because halfway through a routine, a dancer dragged me from my front-row seat up on stage and I became part of the chorus line.

Then, just as I was enjoying the spotlight, my choker exploded and pearls scattered all over the stage. The dancers were forced to break up as they gamely tried to grab pearls as they rolled across the floor.

I didn't have the heart to tell them they were fake.

My English grandmother, May, lived to garden. Her kingdom was an acre of garden enclosed by a high stone wall in a tiny village called Ugborough in South Devon.

Even at 102, she gardened every day, rain or shine. But no matter how dirty the work, Granny would never dream of wearing trousers. She always dressed in tailored skirts or dresses and adored anything with a flowery print.

My mother would comb shops in America to find her something summery and garden-themed and then mail them over. This glorious silk dress was one of Granny's favourites. She loved the fact that the print was not traditional flowers, but dandelions - a weed that wouldn't be tolerated in her garden, yet looked so pretty on her dress.

Ugborough won the title of The Best Kept Village for several years while my grandmother was garden club president. I suspect it was probably helped along by Gran's penchant for prowling the streets to ensure everyone kept up her standards.

When I was a student in Paris, I lived for a year with a family who had an apartment on Avenue de la Grande Armée, just a block away from the Arc de Triomphe.

I arrived with huge suitcases full of vintage dresses Doris felt I was sure to need. One night I was invited to Maxim's by a charming man called Patrick whose father owned a major modelling agency. When I arrived he was entertaining two male models who had just arrived from the United States, so suddenly I had three handsome escorts.

And not only good-looking, but gallant. When I walked in wearing this 1950s party dress, I felt out of place because all the women looked ultra chic in skintight black Azzedine Alaia. But my entourage of gorgeous men immediately made me feel like a million dollars - and reminded me that no one could be overlooked in a dress like this.

It's the last day of 1951 and Emily is standing under the colonnades of the Officers' Club balcony, breathing in the Savannah night air as she enjoys a brief rest from dancing at the New Year's Eve ball.

At nineteen years of age, this feels like her first grown-up ball. All her other dances have been debutante parties, with girls her own age and boys not much older. Here, tonight, she is dancing with soldiers, some of whom have served overseas. Emily has received many admiring looks, and no wonder. Her asymmetrical ball gown of wine-coloured silk taffeta, with its abundant skirt (seventeen yards of fabric altogether - she and her mother measured it three times because they couldn't believe there was so much material) is spectacular and very grown up.

As the band strikes up one of her favourite songs, 'After the Ball' from *Showboat*, she imagines she is a smouldering Ava Gardner as a handsome young officer offers her his arm and leads her back inside to dance away the final hours of the year. The night is still full of promise. The ball is not over yet.

E very woman has had *the* dress. The dress that makes you feel new, animated, happy, a dress that makes anything seem possible, a dress in which you are somehow more yourself than you've ever been before, a dress in which you can now show the world who you really are.

For Hannah Sarah Randall, this bright avocado green wool dress with velvet 'dragon teeth' trim was the dress. Born in the 1840s, she was raised as a Quaker and married a Quaker. Then another Quaker. And then another Quaker. After three marriages, she finally met her true love. However, because he was not a Quaker, Hannah was 'read out' of her Quaker meeting house and shunned by her community in Vermont.

A vivacious, spirited woman, Hannah didn't regret her decision for a moment because she was so in love. With her new husband's encouragement, she also rediscovered her love of fashion and beautiful things after a lifetime of rejecting ostentation.

But her green dress was always her favourite because it represented her first outward expression of freedom. Best of all, it allowed her to sashay in a bustle, the unashamedly erotic cornerstone of a woman's wardrobe by the 1880s. What more could a modern woman want?

My daughter Olivia and I call this our *Roman Holiday* dress. It always transports me back to a perfect day, enjoying a luxuriously long lunch overlooking the Spanish Steps and watching the crowds promenading up and down the Piazza di Spagna. The warm sun on our backs, a glass of chilled pinot grigio in my hand, a limonata in Olivia's, the smell of jasmine in the air, the bells of Trinità dei Monti chiming, I suddenly, joyously, knew that there was no place in the world I'd rather be.

Afterwards, we wandered along Via Condotti to browse in the boutiques: Yves Saint Laurent, Dior, Burberry, Armani, Gucci, Prada, Chanel, Dolce and Gabbana, Valentino. But this Zara dress stood out from all the rest. Heavenly white chiffon with a delicate print of lilies and peonies, it was floaty and feminine, and my eight-year-old partner in crime insisted I try it on. As I pirouetted in front of the mirror, she clapped her hands in delight.

Olivia assures me she will wear this when she's older. I hope that when she does, she remembers our day in Rome.

Doris always loved the fact that the talents of two legendary women came together in this one spectacular 1930s silk thread dress.

It was created by French designer Madeleine Vionnet, known as the queen of the bias cut for inventing the technique of cutting cloth diagonal to the grain of the fabric, enabling it to cling to the body while moving with the wearer. The sleek, body-skimming line of this dress was enhanced by the natural grace of its wearer, former ballerina Lucia Chase, considered by many to be the queen of American ballet.

Lucia Chase co-founded the American Ballet Theatre in 1940, acting as principal dancer and backer. Over the next forty years her drive, ambition and money kept the company going even during the lean years. Under her leadership, the company developed an international reputation and worked with luminiaries such as Rudolf Nureyev, Jerome Robbins, Twyla Tharp and Mikhail Baryshnikov, who succeeded her as director in 1980. Lucia's extraordinary achievements were officially recognised with the United States Medal of Honour.

And many of her extraordinary clothes luckily found their way to Doris, thanks to Lucia's niece and Doris's good friend, Noni Hall.

When Christian Dior launched the first collection of his new fashion house in Paris in 1947, the distinctive hand-span waists above enormous layered skirts scandalised and seduced the fashion world. Inspired by the ring of petals on a flower, it was originally named the Corolle line, but *Harper's Bazaar* editor Carmel Snow famously rechristened it the 'New Look'.

And that it was, in the best possible way. The romantic silhouette Dior had constructed so peerlessly celebrated a woman's shape in a way no one had dared before - and restored much-needed glamor to a grey postwar world.

Dreaming of owning a Dior occupied the minds of every woman who loved fashion. For Ruth Meyer, the dream came true in the form of this glorious ballerina-style cocktail skirt, teamed with a stylish fitted lace top.

It's little wonder that Dior creations from this golden age of fashion are still the stuff that dreams are made of today.

Having spent seven idyllic years in my rustic *manoir* in the Lot region of southwest France, surrounded by chickens, cats, doves and a dog, building my design business, I was restless and ready to move on.

An ad in *The Spectator* caught my eye: 'Writer seeking house to rent in the Lot, France'. This seemed like perfect timing. When I rang, a man introduced himself simply as Sebastian and we agreed to meet for lunch in the village. An outing on a beautiful Easter Sunday was all the excuse I needed to wear my favourite yellow Courrèges trousers and jaunty Versace jacket. The food was good and the company even better as Sebastian regaled me with stories about the London literary scene. Having lived without television and English newspapers for so long, I hadn't heard of any of these people or him - apparently he was a published author - but it didn't matter.

Browsing in a bookshop at Heathrow a few weeks later, I turned a book over to read the blurb and there was Sebastian staring up at me. The book was *Birdsong*, an international bestseller, and my charming lunch companion had of course been Sebastian Faulks.

He didn't end up renting my house, but he did write his next bestseller, *Charlotte Gray*, somewhere nearby in France.

From the stately Waldorf on Park Avenue to the glamorous Adlon of Berlin and London's grand Savoy, New York socialite Miss Wilhelmina Pearson's elegant form graced any ballroom or state room she entered. Always dressed to the nines, she cut a swathe through the crowds in this elegant suit and osprey hat at a gallery opening.

The only daughter of a shipping tycoon, Willy never married, but it was said she never went anywhere without a handsome man on her arm.

A dip in the sea was no picnic for a woman in Victorian times. Just keeping up with all the strict rules of modesty imposed by Queen Victoria would be enough to weigh you down - literally.

Ladies who were daring enough to take the plunge wore heavy dark wool bathing suits - wool being the perfect choice because it remains opaque when wet. Full-length bloomers were topped with a voluminous skirt, often weighted with shot pellets to ensure it didn't float immodestly up around a lady's ears.

To eliminate any risk of a scandalous glimpse of skin, the bather could add dark cotton stockings, shoes laced up the leg and a bathing cap with a brim to hide one's face. A true lady was in no danger of drowning after donning all this clobber, however, as she would partake in only a quick dip - swimming was not for ladies - before climbing chastely back up the steps to her bathing house.

Wheeled bathing houses were rolled down to the water's edge by local boys who were paid a penny farthing for the service. Not surprisingly, there was often a queue of enthusiastic lads jostling to do the job ...

Safaris and big game hunting were all the rage for the rich and powerful in the 1940s. Movies like *Mogambo* starring Clark Gable, Grace Kelly and Ava Gardner, glamorised the idea for mainstream audiences, but of course fashion was already well ahead of the game.

As shocking as it seems today, exotic animal skin was the last word in elegance. And none was considered more glamorous than leopard skin.

First worn in the late 1930s as an ankle-length coat with fashionably wide collar and cuffs, in the 1950s the resourceful Betty Achenbach revamped it into an elegant short cape, hat and bag.

Hardly a typical wedding dress, mind one fit for a demure Quaker bride, this figure-hugging vision of mint lace ruffles raised more than a few eyebrows when Ann Walker wore it down the aisle to marry Dr Louis Bringhurst in June 1936.

But Ann was a free spirit who never followed the flock. She simply thought this was the loveliest dress she had ever seen and therefore the obvious choice for the most important occasion of her life.

Years later when she gave her beloved wedding dress to Doris for the collection, she warned that it had shrunk dramatically after only one wash. So these days it could only be worn by a very slender woman 'without a single lump or bump out of place'.

When you're invited to the races in England by the Sultan of Penang, you have to dress the part. I certainly did my darnedest in a striking red and white embroidered linen dress and matching hat.

Feeling pretty pleased with the results, I decided to go for a bit of a wander. At first I thought it was my head-turning ensemble that was making everyone stop and stare. But then I looked behind me and saw three burly bodyguards following close behind me, furiously chattering into their walkie talkies. Everyone must have assumed I was some rich American heiress!

Rich cream satin with a blush of rose and covered with pearl drops, this heavenly 1950s creation is the work of Ceil Chapman, said to be Marilyn Monroe's favourite designer. Ceil designed for the movies and television, so her everyday clients included stars like Monroe and Deborah Kerr, who was a personal friend. Elizabeth Taylor commissioned Ceil to design her trousseau for her marriage to Conrad 'Nicky' Hilton.

Ceil started out in New York in 1940 with a company called 'Her Ladyship Gowns', with heiress Gloria Vanderbilt as one of her business partners. But the company traded only briefly under that name before becoming 'A Chapman Original', then simply 'Ceil Chapman' as demand for her glamorous designs grew.

An astute businesswoman, Ceil lent her name to advertising luxury products such as Cadillac, which featured models draped over cars wearing stunning Ceil Chapman gowns. Pictured in her design studio, Ceil also appeared in advertisements for Western Union Telegrams and Playtex. She died in the 1970s, but many of her designs live on as sought after collector pieces.

A London friend once invited me as his date to a birthday dinner and was more than a little mysterious on the details. All he would tell me about dress code was that he would be wearing a suit, so I decided to go all out with a sequined gown that's so sleek and sophisticated it looks like Armani. No doubt I'd be overdressed, but I'd been dying to wear it somewhere, and I'd rather dazzle than underwhelm.

My friend collected me in a chauffeur-driven car, nodding approvingly at my dress, and when we pulled up at the swish Dorchester Hotel in Mayfair, I suddenly felt much better. We were ushered inside and taken directly to a private dining room. At the head of the table was a man I recognised immediately from the newspapers, Adnan Khashoggi, the Turkish-Saudi Arabian billionaire businessman. He rose to greet us, smiling warmly. The birthday boy.

Flanking him were some of the most beautiful women I'd ever seen, all wearing haute couture and giving new meaning to the expression 'dripping with diamonds'. I shook my head in wonder - and relief. Thank my lucky stars I took a chance and wore the most dazzling thing I owned.

Glamorous and luxuriantly pink, this 1960s beaded ball gown was worn by a woman who knew more about the law than most lawyers. First the long-time secretary and then the wife of a circuit court judge, Millie was the one person her husband Albert could always rely on to thrash out cases with at the end of the day. Her sharp mind and ability to cut to the nub of an issue helped him keep some of the more difficult aspects of his job in perspective.

When Albert retired, he and Millie travelled regularly to Paris, London, Rome and New York, where she would enjoy scouring the bookshops and shopping for the latest fashions. But Albert never took to retirement and ended up working as a judge into his nineties. Even when Millie became ill, he would still sit by her bedside to talk over his cases with her every night.

This yellow 1940s dress always reminded Doris of Vivien Leigh in *Gone With the Wind* and of a friend 'meeting' the actress when he was on leave from the RAF in London during the Second World War.

He was in a grand hotel bar when he saw this exquisitely beautiful young woman come in with an older woman. He immediately thought she looked familiar, but just couldn't place her so he went up to the bar and blurted out the old line: 'Don't I know you from somewhere?'

Perhaps because he was genuinely nonplussed, the young woman smiled politely and said he might have seen her in a play. He was still not making the connection and, when he offered to buy her and her companion a drink, she declined but gave him two free tickets to a play she was appearing in that week.

It wasn't until she left soon after and he rejoined his party that the penny dropped.

What do you wear to a ball at a palace? Thanks to Doris's love of dressing up - and dressing me up - I never had to worry. When I was invited to the extravagant Black and White Ball at Blenheim Palace in Oxfordshire I was armed with the perfect ensemble, a superbly cut 1930s black lace and jersey couture gown that made me feel like royalty.

Without the confidence it gave me, I might have been tempted to stay at the top of the grand staircase and simply watch the hundreds of strangers gathering for a concert by the Queen's Guard band in the palace courtyard below. Instead, I danced the night away with escorts like the Maharajah of Jaipur.

Truly fit for a princess, this glorious confection of pink silk faille, organdie and tulle, lavishly embroidered with pearl and crystal beads, diamantes and sequins, is every girly-girl's dream dress. The debutante who wore this otherworldly creation certainly must have felt like royalty as she made her grand entrance at the 1962 Veiled Prophet Ball in St Louis, her massive twelve-foot train trailing elegantly behind her, every tiny bead sparkling under the chandeliers.

A tradition dating back to 1878 to celebrate the harvest, every year a debutante is crowned 'Queen of Love and Beauty' at the ball. But a scandal at the 1928 ball cast a long shadow. The intended 'queen' was found to have secretly married several days before, therefore violating the rule that the queen had to be a maiden. Told she was a disgrace to her family and given travelling money 'to be gone', her name was deleted from the St Louis social register.

Surely no such cruel fate befell our mysterious 1962 debutante, 'Miss A', the only hint of her identity handwritten in ink inside her couture gown. Miss A may not have been crowned queen, but anyone wearing this magical dress would surely have had an unforgettable evening …

On my 16th birthday, Doris gave me the choice of anything I wanted from her collection. It was difficult picking one from all my favourites but this dark blue organdie 1950s dress with matching fingerless gloves was the standout.

Such timeless elegance made it the perfect choice for a swanky New Year's Eve ball in Hong Kong almost a decade later. As I was to be escorted by my English cousin Nicholas, I was looking forward to staying at his luxurious apartment on The Peak almost as much as attending the ball. On arrival at Nick's, his amah whisked my precious dress away. It was returned beautifully pressed, with every tiny lace flower standing to attention.

Feeling like a starlet as I draped my wrap around my shoulders, we sped off in Nick's MG to the ball at Repulse Bay. Hosted by the Grenadier Guards in a sprawling colonial-style mansion, a full orchestra played as crowds of beautiful people danced or romanced on the wide verandah or in the beautiful lamplit gardens.

After midnight, four of us squeezed into the MG and roared back up The Peak, stopping to toast the spectacular view with French champagne in paper cups.

My mother's status as a champion tennis player landed her a dream job in Bermuda in 1954.

After seeing her in action at a tennis tournament in Plymouth, an American woman who lived in Bermuda offered to sponsor her visa so she could work at the Coral Beach Club, *the* place to stay in those days.

Her role was to partner up with guests at the club who wanted to play tennis. Tropical weather, swimming, dancing and playing tennis with handsome playboys on immaculate tennis courts lined with pink bougainvillea - nice work if you can get it.

Just before flying out, she bought what was to become a favourite bathing suit at Simpsons on Piccadilly in London. I have a wonderful photograph of her sitting on a rock, her hair blowing in the wind. She looks beautiful, happy - and ready for an adventure.

Dressing in Pucci or Jean Muir just to muck about on your sprawling country estate was nothing out of the ordinary for this English lady.

Arabella loved the tranquillity of the countryside and the chance to ride her beloved horses, while her husband adored living in a 'work of art' filled with priceless furniture and artefacts, and throwing lavish house parties.

But when the marriage ended and Arabella was left alone, she discovered that she much preferred the company of animals to people. Still dressed in exquisite 1960s designer outfits like this, she would be seen roaming the grounds and great halls with a pack of twelve Alsatians.

Diamonds aren't always a girl's best friend.

Simone fell madly in love with a Frenchman who was visiting New York just after the outbreak of the Second World War. He swept her off her feet and plied her with expensive gifts, like this shell pink French lingerie set. Silk of this quality and exquisite cut became impossible to find during the war, but somehow her lover always found something unique to bring her when he came over from France. Then his visits stopped abruptly.

Simone found out later he was one of the wealthiest men in France at the time, but as a Jew he had to go underground to survive. He was saved by a woman who took him into her home and concealed him from the Germans. His rescuer fell in love with him and wanted him to stay with her after the war, but he didn't love her. However, he was so grateful she had saved his life that he promised her he would never marry.

After the war, he wrote to Simone, saying that he would always love her but he couldn't break his vow.

Refusing to wear a bustle could get a girl arrested in the 1880s. But for Mrs Emily Ashley, it was a matter of principle. She and her husband Gilbert ascribed to the Aesthetic Movement, which sought to release society from the prim constrictions and unnatural clutter of Victorian fashion, both in the style of one's home and on one's person.

Emily wasn't a feminist or a suffragette. But she did work tirelessly for children's and women's causes in New York City, and was outspoken on matters of poverty.

While visiting relatives in a small town in Connecticut, Emily was arrested, not for being outspoken, but because she wasn't wearing a corset beneath her dress! It was considered by the town fathers that Mrs Ashley's garb endorsed a style most commonly worn by prostitutes, and she was fined five dollars for the offence. As she heatedly pointed out, five dollars was more than a week's pay for the working poor.

Gilbert, bemused but keen to avoid Emily being arrested once more for striking an officer of the law with her parasol, paid the fine.

As groovy now as it was in the 1960s, this military-style pink wool mini was designed by couturier Guy Meliet. It is just one of many superb designer pieces given to Doris for the collection by her former daughter-in-law, Chesley Larson.

There were no tricksy mother-in-law issues with Doris for Chesley - they were more like best girlfriends. After all, both adored dressing up and were passionate about the collection. And Chesley not only had fabulous taste and a wardrobe to match, but she was also a gifted seamstress who loved helping restore pieces for Doris. The two of them would spend hours talking about clothes and sorting through new pieces as she repaired intricate beading or fixed hems.

Using their favourite garments from the collection, Chesley would create perfect reproductions for herself and Doris to wear. They may not have stretched to matching minis, but I somehow think if Doris had been stepping out in the 1960s she would have loved wearing an outfit like this.

Doris might have been a Quaker, but there was no way she was going to let Quaker modesty about dress or anything else get in the way of her dream wedding dress.

Rebellious as ever, she planned an extravagant gown made of fabric brought over specially from Holland for her big day in 1937. The final touch would be a spectacular eight-foot train but when the Quaker Elder heard of this he said enough is enough.

Knowing Doris all too well though, he wisely came up with a compromise. He asked if Doris would consider meeting him halfway and cutting the extravagant train by half. Doris acquiesced, but of course made up for it in other ways.

Needless to say, she was a beautiful bride.

Great grandmama's Victorian cranberry red bustle dress oversaw many a family gathering and business venture, including the evolution of the family's humble Ricker Inn in Poland Springs into a favourite summer retreat for the rich and famous in the late 1800s. Everyone who was anyone came by coach to be cured by the waters.

A commanding presence, grandmama was actively involved in the family business. The swish of her skirt warned she was approaching on her rounds, issuing orders and keeping an eye out for any employee who might dare to consider allowing shoddy service or any hint of unseemly manners.

My mother's beautiful 1950s cream brocade wedding dress always reminds me of rainy afternoons growing up in Honeymoon Cottage in Pennsylvania. When we were forced to play inside, my sister and I would race up to the attic and dig this glorious treasure out of its storage box, and I would transform myself into the blushing bride, complete with veil and a posy of dandelions. Not so much fun for my sister and brother, however. My sister was always the bridesmaid, never the bride, and my brother was always an English guardsman. I'm not sure why a guardsman, but as long as I was in charge all was right with the world.

For Doris, the dress always reminded her of a male guest's observation in a thank-you note he sent to my grandmother after the wedding, which was held in a marquee in her garden at Devon in 1958:

'I was amused at your remarkable tact in placing the marquee on the soft lawn, having observed the penetrative effect of high heels, enabling husbands to swiftly evade their wives.'

This tiny prairie dress belonged to one of the courageous young pioneer women who followed their husbands into the Wild West to carve out a new life for themselves.

The silk gowns and bustles she wore in the city had no place here. This cotton printed dress was her favourite and only best dress, much loved and mended. Each leftover scrap of fabric used in the making of it was saved and used to let out, mend and patch her precious dress over the years. Whenever she wanted to spruce it up, a fragment of lace or ribbon she might have squirreled away would be added to the sleeve and collar. Only one petticoat was worn underneath in summer, more in winter to keep warm, and the skirt was slightly shorter than was the fashion, to avoid the inevitable wear and tear of dust and mud.

To endure the hardships of frontier life, women had to be as strong, resilient and resourceful as their men, and any talent for mending, crocheting, darning and sewing became a survival skill.

'Honeymoon Cottage' was a sweet stone mill tucked below the hills in a picturesque valley with a stream wandering through. The cottage belonged to a Quaker family in rural Pennsylvania who loaned it to young Quaker couples needing a place to stay during their honeymoon.

I have a lovely old photograph of Doris and Howard standing outside the cottage's front door. Doris is wearing a sweet cotton print dress covered with sprigs of tiny flowers, and she's showing Howard a kitten she found. They look so young and so in love.

When I turned six, I shared the excitement of my parents buying their first home. They rang Doris and Howard to tell them the news about this quaint country cottage they'd found that would be so perfect for raising me and my brother and sister. After a few minutes of conversation, my parents realised they had fallen in love with Doris and Howard's 'Honeymoon Cottage'.

Hand-made lace over fine cotton, exquisite spider's-web embroidery covering every button, this Edwardian dress is an ethereal masterpiece, and a clear indication of the wealth and position of its lucky owner.

Indeed, in 1910 Bert Bailey's mother was a resident of Pennsylvania's exclusive 'Main Line', which came to refer to the collection of sprawling estates that sprang up along the route of the old main railway line.

Her family lived a life of absolute privilege, helped along by a battery of servants, including upstairs and downstairs maids, a cook, laundress, chauffeur and gardener. Most importantly, this Edwardian beauty had her own personal maid and the services of the best seamstress and latest fashions from Paris and London to ensure she was always head and shoulders above the rest.

In my twenties I was working at a London art gallery when I fell madly in what I thought was love with a gorgeous Canadian bon vivant called Henry. A passionate collector of Impressionist art and Georgian furniture, he would spoil me whenever he was in town, squiring me to all the finest restaurants and then on to dancing at the famous Annabel's nightclub - in those days the exclusive playground of the rich and famous.

Best of all, Henry was one of those rare men who loved to shop, and on one memorable occasion he whisked me off on his private jet for a day of shopping in New York City. On the return flight, I boarded wearing a new flame-red Gianfranco Ferre outfit I had been treated to that day, thinking we were returning to London for dinner. But instead Henry took me to a luxurious hotel on the island of Anguilla in the West Indies for a few days of R&R.

Even now, when I breathe in sea air, I am reminded of that crazy lady-in-red day of jetsetting.

S ome dresses are so beautiful that sometimes just owning them is enough. Doris's mother, Faith, always longed to wear this exquisite salmon-pink silk evening dress but had never found the right special occasion for it.

As a doctor's wife, Faith was often required to act as hostess, but as their small house had no suitably formal rooms that usually meant she would have to entertain guests at their country club instead.

In the early days of their marriage, she would go off with an estate agent and look at grand old houses. But any that fit her modest price bracket always needed huge amounts of restoration the newlyweds simply couldn't afford. So instead, the young couple bought a house with three rooms downstairs where they could host informal get-togethers. After a pot-luck dinner, everyone would sit around and chat. Many fine times were had, but there was no room for formality.

Doris doesn't remember her mother ever being dressed up in a long gown for a fancy affair held in their home. But her mother kept this dress anyway, just in case.

This stylish 1920s yellow silk outfit and matching
cloche hat belonged to Mildred Davis, an American
woman whose lifelong dream was to travel the world. But
Mildred was one of those people who could never say no
and instead she spent her life loyally caring for a procession
of ailing relatives.

Unable to spend her hard-earned allowance on travel, she
bought the most beautiful clothes she could afford. Doris
said clothes were the only joy and colour in Mildred's life.

But Mildred could at least still dream of wearing them all
on a slow boat to somewhere exotic …

Feeling like an extra in a James Bond movie, I had to pinch myself as I was escorted to a table at Le Casino de Monte-Carlo in the summer of 1986.

In a shimmering black and silver gown with a silver dollar sign clasp, and a glass of Dom Pérignon in my hand, I might have looked like I belonged, but I was making it up as I went along. I had been invited to the casino as the personal assistant to a Parisian art dealer to help him entertain some of his wealthy clients. It was job I'd had for only a day and I remember trying very hard to appear sophisticated among this glittering throng.

Thanks to a fabulous dress, a little French champagne and beginner's luck at the roulette wheel, I think I pulled it off.

When Lida Mae wore her swishy new black velvet gown with daring cutaway shoulders to a country club dance in the 1930s, she felt truly glamorous for the first time in her life. Thanks to her newfound confidence, she had a magical evening dancing almost exclusively with the most handsome man in the room.

Lida always remembered the dress with special affection and a wicked gleam in her eye. As she confided to Doris, she always thought the effect of the barely-there sleeves, fastened in only one spot at the shoulder, was deliciously 'titillating'.

B elgian silk jacquard with a subtle print of lily of the valley, gathered together into an extravagant bow at the back and a long train, my wedding dress was a masterpiece of construction. It was also very heavy and as the guests gathered in the heat under the marquee on my English godmother Jill's Devon estate, I remember thinking that the spring blossoms on the wedding cake weren't the only things starting to wilt.

I fervently wished I'd followed my instincts and had a much shorter dress - a mini with a long train was all the rage then. I'd also wanted to wear a padded bra to create a more dramatic cleavage. But I'd listened to my mother's advice on both counts to avoid the risk of offending my elderly relatives.

Years later, I wonder whether my doubts about the dress masked something else. Sadly, the marriage didn't last. But the dress has stood the test of time and I can appreciate its beauty now. Perhaps my mother was right.

The day Doris received her invitation to my wedding in England in 1989, she promptly called from across the Atlantic to accept. For the next two months, I received excited notes from her, telling me about the wardrobe she planned to bring.

In one letter she asked me if an enormous hat with arcing ostrich plumes might be too large for the church, as she had recently read an etiquette book which stipulated no woman should wear a hat that might block the view of the person seated behind. Another letter asked if a dinner at the local pub might give her the opportunity to wear the 1930s magenta taffeta skirt with hot pink sash she had lately acquired.

Nevertheless, I was still unprepared for the sight of Doris alighting from the train in Barnstaple, a sleepy little town in the heart of Lorna Doone country. Sporting a wide-brimmed hat in bold black and white zebra stripe, she was waving her black vintage parasol authoritatively at the overwhelmed train attendant trying to gather all her bags and hat boxes together.

Indeed, the godmother of the bride had arrived - in her fashion.

This stylish 1960s silk brocade dress belonged to a wealthy stage actress who loved to shop for exotic fabrics on her frequent travels abroad. She discovered this brocade woven with a distinctive pattern of Cedars of Lebanon in a market in Damascus and took it to Paris to have it made into a dress, with no less than eighty covered buttons down the front.

Making an entrance for her was all about the detail and wearing something that was truly unique.

Only a thoroughly Modern Millie who could dangle a long ivory cigarette holder as smoothly as she drove her sleek powder-blue Cadillac could wear this dress with confidence. Determined to raise both his daughters to be free spirits, Helen's father bought one of the first cars in Rhode Island and taught his girls to drive. He insisted they go to college and get jobs out there in the real world. Helen did just that, and ended up vice-president of a cosmetics company.

Helen never married - the idea simply never appealed to her. But she did become the favourite aunt of all her sister's children. She taught her nieces and nephews all the dances from her day - the Black Bottom and the Charleston - as well as how to drive. The motto she lived by was 'Work hard and be sensible, but never forget to have fun'.

This was one of Doris's favourite flapper dresses because it is so marvellous to swirl around in and seems to have a magical effect on its wearer. As she put it:

'Everyone who puts this dress on acquires a kind of 1920s attitude. A widowed friend of mine wore it and as soon as her very handsome and thoughtful escort for the evening saw her, he dashed out and bought her a cigarette holder and bangles to complete the effect. She was tickled pink over this and had quite the glint in her eye - as you would!'

My English grandmother May met my grandfather in Egypt in the 1920s when she went over to visit her eldest brother. As my grandfather worked for the British Government, he had his own car and driver. It was a sleek black roadster, but my grandmother remembers it was always breaking down, usually somewhere remote in the desert.

Granny was very independent, so whenever she felt restless she'd borrow the car and roar off to explore or visit the local markets, returning with a pile of beautiful carpets sticking out of the boot. To protect herself from the elements, Granny always wore a lightweight linen duster buttoned up under her chin, with either gloves or leather wrist bands over her cuffs to prevent the sand from riding up her sleeve in dust storms. Wearing a sturdy but stylish hat, secured with a scarf, and her favourite yellow Bakelite driving goggles, she was ready for anything.

Just like a feisty heroine in a Hercule Poirot mystery, Granny was not only impeccably dressed but always prepared for the next adventure.

Doris's friend Barbara loved clothes and adored dressing up in the latest fashion, something that didn't always sit well with her fellow Quakers.

After one very conservative soul took her to task for wearing a snazzy fur-trimmed dress and matching hat to a Germantown meeting in the 1950s, her response was, 'Only the Lord will have to worry about whether this is appropriate or not'.

As Louisa May Alcott proved in *Little Women*, when in need of a special 'new' dress, a girl need go no further than the attic and the trunks of clothes inherited from grandma or great grandma for a precious piece of damask or a gown one could reinvent.

In the 1890s women had to know how to sew, and many would have spent hours with their needle and thread drawing inspiration from *Godey's Lady's Book* featuring the latest looks from Paris.

Luscious silk brocade with an enormous pouffe of a bow to accentuate the bustle and a long train, the original version of this grand wedding dress featured fashionable leg-of-mutton sleeves and an apron-like panel over the front of the skirt when it was first worn in 1883. When the next bride in the family raided the attic almost twenty years later she replaced the puffy sleeves with loose lace sleeves and removed the apron. In such modern times as 1899, the young bride also made the decolletage a little more daring.

In either form, no bride could fail to cause a ripple of envy among her friends as she walked down the aisle.

After a fairytale week in Monaco for a lavish wedding, staying at a swanky five-star hotel, I had come back down to earth with a thump. As I looked around my dingy budget hotel room, at least there was one bright spot. An art dealer at the wedding had offered me a job in Paris, so I sought him out.

The job as his personal assistant sounded too good to be true - spend another week in Monaco meeting some of his clients and then travel back to Paris with him to start my job in earnest. I happily accepted and the next day Henri gave me an incredible amount of money to shop for a designer wardrobe, telling me to think of it as my 'uniform' for our week of entertaining. I had a glorious day shopping at all the best Monte Carlo boutiques, which is where I bought this green Guy Laroche ensemble.

I was young and naïve to say the least, but when a concerned friend pulled me aside and told me some home truths about Henri, I thought it was time to get out of town.

I took the Guy Laroche with me though - a fair day's pay for a fair day's work, sort of, and a lesson learned.

This 1840s lavender taffeta crinoline was worn by a young bride as she struggled to adjust to married life in St Louis. Raised in a closeknit family in Philadelphia, Isabella was pining for their company and the city she knew and loved so well. Her wealthy husband James adored her and tried everything he could to help his wife overcome her homesickness.

One day he suggested a present to cheer her up, a carved rosewood parlour set made by a famous cabinet maker from her home town. Isabella was delighted with the idea and thirty custom-made pieces were duly ordered. After months of painstaking work, the superbly crafted furniture was delivered by barge from Philadelphia to the Allegheny Mountains, then by ox-cart over the mountains and then by steamer down the Mississipi to St Louis.

Several months after the parlour set had been installed and admired by all and sundry, Isabella announced that it just wouldn't do. She loved James, but she could not be happy living so far from her family. James knew when to admit defeat so they moved to Philadelphia, where they lived happily ever after - without the rosewood parlour set.

When I was living in London in the early 1980s, I was looking for an excuse to wear this wild Ann Pakradooni lace pantsuit when some friends invited me to a party just around the corner in South Kensington.

We walked into this enormous room which was all white - white walls, ceiling, huge white leather modular sofa and chairs. There were three guys with perfectly groomed hair dressed in white pantsuits, their shirts unbuttoned down to a scarily low point, lounging on the sofa.

Nobody seemed to know what they were doing there and I remember thinking how much they looked like the Bee Gees. I later found out it was them, but I still think my white outfit outdazzled theirs.

A lice, better known as AJ, was a Bryn Mawr classmate Doris remembers fondly as 'a true maverick who looked at the world with humorous and sometimes cockeyed glasses'.

'AJ was extremely beautiful, lovely to look at, with bright red hair, bright blue eyes, a glowing complexion and a kind of Mae West figure. And her clothes were always beautiful.' Like this peach silk-ribbon 'wiggle dress' she wore in the 1950s.

Doris loved that AJ lived to break convention, even small ones, like wearing ankle socks with high heels. The former were customary at college, but wearing them with high heels was considered 'beyond the pale'.

When the girls graduated, Doris received three treasured books from her parents. AJ's very wealthy parents fought over what to give her and her father finally settled on a convertible. Her mother was so jealous that she had been outdone that she took one of AJ's delicate diamond rings and traded it for one with a much larger emerald-cut diamond. As you do.

In the 1930s debutantes as sophisticated and stylish as Martha Estabrook's daughter Emmeline were not interested in blending into the crowd in predictable white organdie. Instead, she chose a daring chartreuse gown with a matching jacket and mink collar.

As was the custom, her mother had thrown an afternoon tea party for her own friends, followed by a dinner dance for her daughter's friends to kick up their heels. Emmeline sensibly left her jacket on for the more sedate tea party, but when she removed it for the dance she discovered that the back was much lower than she remembered.

All the better she thought, but next time she'd be prepared with a cleverly constructed brassiere that didn't ruin the effect - and prepared too for the temptation of some dance partners to explore the possibilities her daring backline presented.

The comment had been an arrow to her heart. Lulu had not meant to eavesdrop, but the secret was out: the family of her son's bride-to-be was concerned she might spoil the wedding by wearing one of her dowdy outfits.

A sensible Quaker who had put her money into good causes rather than good clothes, Lulu decided a day at Bergdorf Goodman in New York, rediscovering her taste for beautiful clothes she had had neither the time nor inclination to indulge in while raising her children, was overdue. Returning home with an arsenal of designerwear, she felt victorious.

On the eve of the big day, Lulu made sure every last little detail was perfect before going upstairs to dress in her sensational new black velvet gown, with its latticed devoré sleeves in the latest 1930s style, liberally sprinkled with diamantes.

Every woman's worst nightmare came true however as the bodice became stuck over her hips. 'But I got into it when I bought it in New York!' she sobbed to her husband.

Deftly loosening a button hidden from view, he freed Lulu to duly impress their guests with her newfound sophistication and poise.

E very woman dreams of wearing a Christian Dior original. Ruth Meyer lived the dream, even being fitted personally at the Dior salon in Paris. The result was this breathtaking champagne-pink slipper satin gown, the ideal ensemble for a dinner reception at the White House, hosted by the President and First Lady, Franklin and Eleanor Roosevelt.

As the daughter of Eugene Meyer, owner and publisher of *The Washington Post* and head of the World Bank, Ruth needed an extensive couture wardrobe for such glittering events and the many dinner parties her parents hosted at their palatial home in Washington. From an early age, she was enlisted to greet visitors while her parents were still dressing. Ruth always felt this was a ploy by her parents to help her learn the social graces. It certainly worked, as she became renowned for being the perfect hostess, someone who could make anyone feel at ease, from ambassadors and Supreme Court judges to artists and performers.

At her spectacular coming-out party in 1939 it was said that everybody who was anybody in Washington was invited. But for Ruth, it was just a gathering of her extended family.

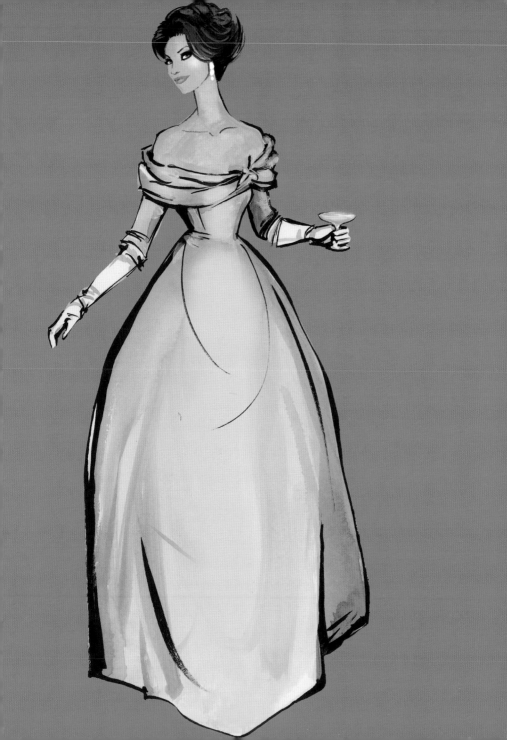

As a student at a women's college in the 1950s, there were many rules to follow and Catherine Carlisle always seemed to be bending them. A darkly beautiful young woman with laughter in her eyes, there was always an air of mischief about her.

One of the quaint rules of Wellesley College was that when a student entertained a gentleman in her room, the door must be open and three feet had to be on the floor at all times. Just as stringent was the rule to dress in formalwear for dinner every evening, and to be punctual.

In summer, Catherine loved to take a refreshing dip in the pond that lay in the middle of the campus. One balmy June evening, however, waylaid chatting to a particularly handsome young man, she found herself running so late for dinner that she had to pull her watermelon silk evening gown over her wet bathing suit, twist her wet hair into ringlets, and make a dash for it.

It made for a rather uncomfortable dinner. No one in the hall guessed at her predicament, or why she kept erupting into laughter - no one except the handsome young man in question. His name was Harold Brownlee, and they were married the following June.

The beloved daughter of a grand family in St Louis, Mary Elizabeth Davies loved city life and was accustomed to dressing in the latest fashion. None of that mattered to Charles Rhodes, the handsome country gentleman from Kentucky who fell in love with her and won her hand.

When they became engaged, Elizabeth asked her father if she could visit her fiancé's family and friends before the wedding. To her surprise her father said: 'No. You have decided to marry Charles Rhodes. This is the most important decision in your life. You will meet, and learn to love and adjust to his family and friends in Danville when you get there. There is no point in going now'.

Undaunted, Elizabeth went on with having her trousseau made in Paris and St Louis, and arrived with trunks of exquisite gowns suitable for grand parties in St Louis but not so country Danville. The reaction of Charles's family on her arrival of polite, but barely masked astonishment, made it all worthwhile. And at least Mary was assured of always being the best-dressed woman in town.

P aris in the springtime is a wonderful place to fall in love, but I think winter is just as romantic, especially when it snows.

One snowy day stands out in my memory, thanks to a handsome Frenchman who was out to impress me. After a wonderful lunch at one of the most famous restaurants in Paris, La Tour d'Argent, I thought my companion had done a fine job. In all my thirty years, I couldn't remember a better meal.

Admiring the spectacular view of the Seine from our table and the snowflakes floating down around Notre Dame, we were suddenly inspired to see the snow falling over Paris from another landmark, the Eiffel Tower. As we rose to leave, a sea of tail-coated waiters parted before us, and I was helped into my luxurious faux fur Anne Klein coat. The matching hat not only looked fabulous, but it did its job protecting my ears from the icy cold as we hailed a taxi.

The snowflakes danced around us as we emerged from the tower lift, settling on the shoulders of my coat. The Frenchman lightly brushed them away and took my gloved hand in his as we leant over the railings to gaze at Paris laid out in all its winter white glory.

Embroidered with 'spider's web' panels, this 1960s yellow and white cotton mini and matching jacket has rocked more than a few gala events in its time and has many admirers. They include Niccole Warren, from the ABC's popular *Collectors* television show, who wore it to the 2008 Logie Awards.

I am especially fond of it because it always reminds me of my lovely, but dizzy blonde college roommate. One day when we were driving past fields of cotton on the plains of Savannah, Georgia, she said: 'Wow, look at all that wool.'

In her honour, I always refer to this as my 'cotton-wool' dress.

An impossibly intricate masterpiece of hand-crocheted lace, this ivory tea-gown was worn by Charlotte Glenn as part of her trousseau when she married John McMullin in 1904.

The designer's label, hand-stitched inside the waistband, reads 'Dunleavy, Cincinnatti, Ohio', the city's leading dressmaker at the turn of the century. An Irish immigrant, Anna Dunleavy graduated from a humble saleslady selling expensive fabrics to rich clients to running a dressmaking business from her home in 1889. Five years later she had a booming business, employing twelve assistants.

Although she was a gifted seamstress, Anna could not read or write. Undaunted by this, her thriving business allowed her to travel to Europe regularly to buy expensive fabrics and keep ahead of the latest fashions in Paris.

But in order to create a dress like this Anna would have employed the talents of local Irish lace makers. As Irish immigrant men flocked to the city to work in the mines in the 1900s, their womenfolk often ended up working in sweatshops for a pittance. Thanks to the traditional lacemaking skills many brought with them, Cincinnati soon became as renowned for its lace production as its steel.

This elegant beaded flapper dress was just one of many magnificent period dresses that made the indomitable Doris the envy of all her companions on a cruise around the Greek islands.

When wealthy friends invited my godmother and her husband Howard to join them on a luxury cruise in the 1960s, Doris was about to politely decline because they simply couldn't afford such luxuries. But Howard had been given some shares so they decided to splurge. Sadly, their windfall didn't stretch to buying Doris the dazzling new wardrobe she knew all the other women would be showing off at every opportunity.

But Doris had an even better idea for stealing the limelight at the inevitable parade of fancy cocktail parties, dances and dinner at the captain's table. Using her favourite historical characters as inspiration, she chose the most fabulous dresses and accessories from her vintage collection so that every night she made a grand entrance as a glamorous time traveller from a different decade.

As she proudly wrote later, 'No one, no matter what they had paid for their clothes from the best shops in Philadelphia, had anything more beautiful than what I wore'.

D og-tired from filling a massive order for Galeries Lafayette in Paris for a line of lampshades I had designed, I politely declined when a friend invited me out to lunch in London.

But he was determined, arguing that I had to eat some time and clearly needed cheering up. My resolve lasted all of two minutes, and an hour later I found myself thoroughly enjoying a lavish lunch at the Berkeley Hotel. Good food and great company did wonders for my mood.

After lunch, he convinced me to accompany him to Harrods on an errand and then cajoled me into trying on a sharp and sassy Thierry Mugler suit that had caught my eye, all pleats and tucks, cinched waist, flared hips and a daringly short skirt. My friend smiled wickedly as the sales assistants fussed over me, clearly thinking he was my sugar daddy.

This impression was cemented when he told them to put the outfit and a pair of Versace shoes and handbag on his account. I had to politely decline, but he insisted I take the suit as a gift. He sure knew how to lift a girl's spirits.

But when the cheque came for my lampshades, I went back and treated myself to the Versace shoes and bag.

Despite a chorus of disapproval, Olive Zug wore this daring beaded flapper dress when she married William Forsythe in 1922. Olive had planned a Christmas wedding and a dress that some conservative members of the family sniped was better suited as a tree decoration.

When her father died suddenly just weeks before the wedding, the same relatives said she should postpone the wedding, that it was not done to get married at Christmas time and she shouldn't wear a dress as daring as this. But Olive's father had been looking forward to this wedding almost as much as she had, and had left his beloved daughter in no doubt that he wholeheartedly approved of both her choice of husband and her dress.

So the wedding went ahead just as he would have wished - and soon after brides-to-be all over town wanted a dress as stunning as this one.

When the Metropolitan Opera opened in New York City in 1883, a wealthy socialite rose to the occasion in this splendid black satin, lace and jet-beaded gown, complete with a magnificent bustle and train.

For the centenary celebrations in 1983, the dress was invited back, along with Doris, to provide in her words, 'a vivid, living glimpse' of the grand Victorian fashion on show that first opening night.

On the night, things didn't quite go to plan. Doris's hair, no matter how she piled it on her head, just wouldn't sit right. It simply had to be perfect, and it was, after a dozen or so attempts. But by then she was running dreadfully late, and arrived just as the curtain was about to go up. All opportunity for a photograph of her grand entrance had been lost.

That's not to say Doris didn't make her presence felt. Facing the patrons in her row, she inched her way along, apologising as she went - completely oblivious to the fact that her bustle was thumping into the backs of the heads of those in the front row. Perhaps a few took their revenge at intermission as her train was stood on more than once. But at least she did get her photograph taken for posterity.

This striking silk pink-and-white striped dress belonged to a young American woman who lived a very glamorous life in Paris and whose wardrobe was the envy of all her friends.

When she married a man from an aristocratic family, his mother insisted on buying her new daughter-in-law designer dresses she felt were more suitable for her social position. When the newlyweds moved to Venezuela in the 1960s, she gave her a huge wardrobe full of new designer gowns from couturier Guy Meliet. Any mother-in-law who does that is a keeper.

Young Eleanor Andrews wore this flowered chiffon to a 1935 wedding and had such a wonderful time that she treasured the dress for its happy memories for the rest of her life.

Eleanor's grandfather owned an antique store in New York and put her mother and aunt to work there to learn the trade. But Eleanor said they learned even more about life and how to treat people from him. When her mother started working at the store he told her that when the sandwiches and pies were brought in for lunch, she was to say she was too full to eat the pie. The unwanted slice of pie could then go to the office boy her grandfather suspected was not getting enough to eat. Eleanor said that same boy grew up to head one of the city's largest and most successful auction houses. He may not have known about this act of kindness but for her grandpapa it was reward enough that his charge had learned his trade so well.

When Doris met Eleanor, she was ninety-three, and while she still loved beautiful clothes, she was infamous for wearing a baseball cap to functions.

Annie Potts was always delightfully herself and said precisely what she thought. It was one of the many reasons Charles Jordan adored her and made her his wife.

After their wedding in 1910 Charles took Annie to Newfoundland to meet her mother-in-law, who had a reputation for being a bit of a tartar. Dressed in her best pink silk gown, Annie was also on her best behaviour and everything flowed along smoothly until the meal was over and the senior Mrs Jordan announced, 'Now that we are through with our lunch, it is time for us all to take naps'.

Annie spoke up and said, 'But Mrs Jordan, you need to know that I never take a nap in the daytime'.

Mrs Jordan looked stern and said, 'My dear, when you know me better, you will know that everyone does as I say'.

Without a blink, Annie replied just as directly, 'Well, before we know each other better, perhaps it's time to do as I say'.

There was a very awkward silence and then mother looked at her son and said, 'She reminds me of me at that age'. Mrs Jordan Senior might even have smiled. And young Mrs Jordan did not take a nap.

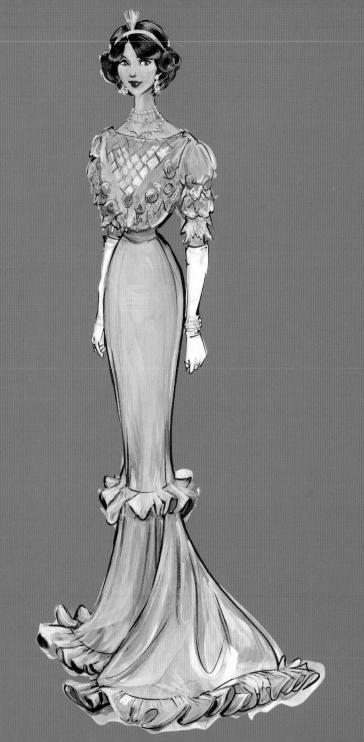

When I was living in London in the 1990s, a dashing
Englishman swept me off my feet. After a whirlwind
romance, he asked me to his 40th birthday party at a
fancy nightclub.

The night before the big event he turned up with a present,
this slinky mini-dress he had bought me on one of his
business trips to Paris. He said he couldn't wait to show me
off to his friends and insisted I wear it to the party. I was
a bit unsure as it was very short and daring and I had the
impression his friends were more like the pearls and tweed
set. But I loved it and I was young and naïve.

The party was wonderful at first, but I began to wonder why
people were coming up and congratulating me. It turned out
they had mistaken me for his fiancée. He had been leading a
double life and fooling us both. What a cad. I met up with
his 'other' fiancée and we dumped him together.

But I kept the dress - a reminder to be more careful
next time …

M ade in Park Lane in London in 1900 for my great grandmother, my mother wore this Belle Epoque silk and lace tea gown to a historical-themed function at the Philadephia Art Museum.

Her dinner companion for the evening was an up-and-coming singer who charmed her. His name was Luciano Pavarotti.

Kathleen Price was a woman of many talents, not the least of which was an eye for style. She adored ballroom dancing and designed her dresses with dancing in mind, even her day dresses. A 1950s original by Miami designer David Roth, with a gloriously full skirt of navy blue broderie anglaise over dusty pink silk is a case in point. As Doris rightly describes it, 'a flirtatious dress'.

While Kathleen made many fabulous dresses for herself and Doris over the years, she loved combing the great stores in Los Angeles and San Francisco like I. Magnin & Company and The White House for finds like this.

Kathleen was also a voracious reader and witty letter writer. But her real gift was singing, and she had perfect pitch. She could sing everything from show tunes to operatic arias by Bizet, Mozart, Puccini and Wagner. Doris recalled that Kathleen would sometimes go to the piano to check a bird's pitch and follow with a spontaneous imitation of the song.

David Roth
Originals
made in miami

While studying in Paris, despite promising my mother otherwise, I loved taking off alone to places I'd never been. One day I jumped on to a train and headed east to Brindisi to catch a ferry to Corfu.

Having packed only a few cute but flimsy cotton dresses, I almost froze on the ferry ride over until I managed to borrow a sweater from some American students. Like me, they had no real plans except to soak up the sun and take each day as it came. And there is no place more magical and romantic than Corfu to do just that.

One morning we decided to hire scooters to explore the island. Impractical as ever, I wore a purple crocheted mini dress I'd bought from a local market stall. Off we set, me with one arm around the waist of my handsome new friend, Philip, the other hanging on to a basket laden with cheese, olives, bread and rosé.

While I don't remember writing anything too spicy in my journal about my Corfu trip, when Doris finished reading it, all she said was 'Wow!'

Betty Black wore this rose-coloured velvet dress to a grand afternoon tea party hosted by her parents to show off their grown-up daughter to their friends before she went off to college in the 1930s.

One guest arrived late, a distinguished elderly retired Harvard professor who was almost as renowned for being more than a little absent-minded when it came to his social life than for being a brilliant scholar.

When he arrived in the entrance hall to the mansion, coat on his arm, he'd obviously thought he'd been invited to a wake, demanding loudly: 'Where's the casket?'

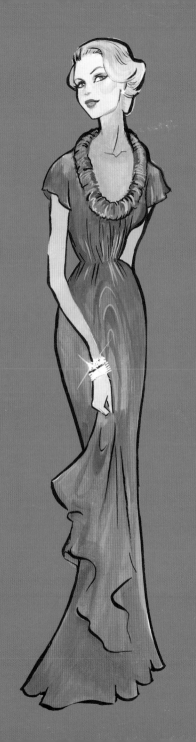

As flamboyant and daring as its owner, this black Balenciaga original was made to party. But it almost missed its opportunity one night when Ellie Parker was invited to a black and white-themed ball in New York.

Told by some mischievous soul that it was a costume affair, Ellie and her date hit on a brilliant idea and turned up in Snoopy costumes. Peering out from under their huge black and white heads, they saw everyone else wearing super glamorous black and white ballgowns and tuxes, and realised they had been had.

After dashing home and changing, when they returned everyone was talking about the mystery guests who turned up in Snoopy outfits. No one knew who they were - and they would hardly suspect anyone who stepped out in Balenciaga.

T his 1970s multi-coloured embroidered kaftan from South Africa belonged to a free spirit who was determined to change the world, or at least make it a little better place to live in.

As her parents worked for an international aid organisation, Asha spent her childhood travelling the world, from the streets of Bombay to Marrakesh. Inspired by her parents' work, she decided to join the World Health Organisation as a field doctor. Stationed in Africa for many years, she was a favourite among her nieces and nephews. After all, no one else at school had home movies for show-and-tell of giraffes and elephants roaming in their auntie's backyard.

In 1946 Japan, a twelve-year-old boy with the customary shaven head of all schoolboys was constantly surrounded by courtiers ready to grant his every wish. But seated next to Crown Prince Akihito was someone who he came to rely on even more, a tall, angular Western woman, often dressed in this tailored suit the colour of the pine trees on the southern slopes of Mount Fuji.

Having decided that his son needed to learn the English language and the ways of Western democracy, Emperor Hirohito had chosen Mrs Vining, a refined and educated American widow in her mid-forties, to fulfil that role.

Over the next four years, Mrs Vining taught the Crown Prince English, played tennis with him, joined the family on outings and even introduced him to one of the most Western games of all, Monopoly. Long after Mrs Vining ended her posting, the Crown Prince and his mother the Empress would visit her in America and they remained lifelong friends.

Doris always said Mrs Vining's life reminded her a little of the story of 'Anna and the King of Siam' Hollywood reinvented as the musical, *The King and I*.

In the late 1990s a lucky friend of mine was invited to Paris for a weekend at the Ritz. After a spectacular high tea on arrival, her wealthy friend suggested she could buy anything she wanted from the boutiques in the hotel. With outfits by every possible French designer the choice was not easy, but she finally settled on this knockout Herve Leger suit and matching shoes.

As she was dressing for dinner, a package was delivered to her room. Inside the stylish black and gold gift box was the distinctive cobalt blue handbag covered in gold cherubs she had admired earlier but, having decided not to be greedy, did not add to her list.

It just goes to show that a little restraint can sometimes pay off.

The ivory gown fitted like a second skin, fluid silk-satin cut on the bias to skim her hips, with a cream Belgian lace overlay, and a long flowing train. Her wedding gown was signature Chanel, a sculptural vision with voluminous sleeves and a tiny belt at the back to give this 1930s Boston bride an understated edge. To complement the simple elegance of the dress, her hair was styled to softly frame her face and decorated with orange blossoms, a symbol of everlasting love.

As the bride waited for her father to finish polishing his new Cadillac Twelve for its maiden journey to the chapel, she wished her mother had been alive to share this moment. Her mother would have loved the planning and her dress, having been a devotee of Gabrielle 'Coco' Chanel and her maxim that 'Simplicity is the keynote of all true elegance'.

At the last minute, she added her mother's favourite earrings - the only tangible way she could keep her mother close on this, her day of days.

R enowned seamstress Kate Ludwig was the first port of call for any woman even thinking of marriage in Boalsburg, Pennsylvania, in 1912.

So when the time came to plan her own trousseau, Kate was determined to create a masterpiece. She stitched all of her hopes and dreams for the future into a breathtakingly beautiful trousseau of evening wear, intricately embroidered petticoats, camisoles and peignoirs.

One of her favourites was a sylph-like gown of the palest silk, swathed by an overlay of fine, jet-black lace. Perhaps she was trying this on the day before her wedding when she received a letter from her fiancé, abruptly informing her that he had just married someone else.

On the day that was supposed to be her wedding, Kate Ludwig hauled her trousseau up to the attic and hid it in a dark corner in a locked chest. Her trousseau remained untouched for more than eighty years. When it was finally opened, every piece was as perfect as when she had created it. But no wedding dress was ever found.

L ooking for adventure, Jenny decided one gloomy day in 1976 to answer an advertisement in *The Times* for a secretary 'for a diplomat living abroad'. Her application was successful and in next to no time she found herself flying to Jordan to work for the British Ambassador.

Erudite, debonair and with an irresistible twinkle in his eyes, Glencairn was thirty years Jenny's senior but she was immediately impressed by him, just as he was captivated by her beauty, intelligence and willingness to immerse herself in a new culture. They soon fell deeply in love, and several months later he asked her to be his wife.

The daughter of my English godmother, Jenny returned home with Glencairn to be married in her parents' garden in Devon. Jenny was certain this cream duchesse satin gown was the perfect choice for her big day. She was even more certain she had found the great love of her life.

It was the start of a long and happy marriage. Together, they had two children and travelled the world, making frequent trips to exotic locations in Asia in search of the indigo plant - Jenny's academic specialty and other passion in life.

Throughout the 1920s a glamorous Philadelphian made an annual pilgrimage from New York to London just to shop. The high point was visiting the famous Liberty store on Regent Street to pick up some must-have items like this intricately embroidered and smocked tan silk pongee dress.

Young Edith was just one of Liberty's eclectic and elite clientele, ranging over the years from Marcel Proust - who always bought his silk ties there - Oscar Wilde and Isadora Duncan to Gilbert and Sullivan, who dressed their casts in Liberty ensembles, no less. Liberty's clothing defined art nouveau fashion; indeed, in Italy, Art Nouveau was known as 'Stile Liberty'.

When Doris asked Edith years later if this transatlantic shopping spree was unusual for a young woman at the time, especially given the Wall Street crash at the end of the decade, Edith replied: 'Oh no, dear. That was what you did. Everyone came home with a Liberty of London dress every year. That's why mine all had dates. This is my 1922 one.'

Perhaps not everyone, but lucky for some.

B etty Herman discovered very early on that her mother-in-law was not as 'proper' as her own mother. For starters, her mother-in-law had a roadster she loved to roar around in and would let her only son, Harry, drive it.

When Harry and Betty were courting in the 1930s, he loved to speed up her parents' driveway and blow the horn to alert his fiancée to come out. Betty's mother was horrified that he didn't come to the door to call for her. But not as horrified as on their wedding day.

On the big day, Harry filled up the boot with bootleg whisky and got stopped by the police. They confiscated it and Harry spent his wedding night in a prison cell.

As the wife of the American Ambassador to Luxembourg, Betsy Harvey's social life was hectic in the late 1950s and early 1960s. But the annual reception at the Grand Duchess's Palace was the undoubted highlight of her social calendar. In 1961, she wrote to a friend back in America:

'The Palace Reception was beautiful, as always. I wore my gold sari dress and had many compliments. It was nice to know more faces this time, although the party gets larger and larger (also longer, which is harder on the feet). The Danish ambassador in scarlet and gold with a shock of white hair is still the most beautiful, although a magnificent, tall British brigadier in a red mess jacket runs a close second. Among the ladies the most striking, for two years running now, have been the Spanish delegates, with black hair piled high over aristocratic features and the most outstandingly chic dresses to set off quite devastating figures.'

This spectacular silk 'sari dress', designed by Madame Jacquemin, was surely just as outstandingly chic. Betsy may not have realised how stunning she looked in it, but it's certain her husband, the Danish ambassador and the British brigadier did.

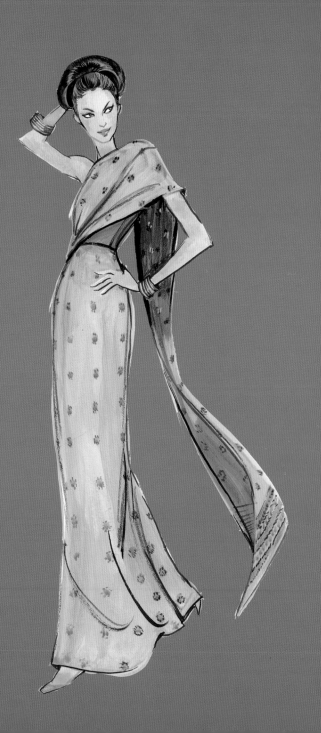

E rnestine Hartley chose traditional white for her wedding
gown so that she could wear her grandmother's
Chantilly lace wedding veil. Her dress was made of the finest
silk, metres of it, with an extravagantly long train that floated
behind her as she glided down the aisle.

Ever practical, Ernestine cleverly timed her Edwardian
wedding to her beloved James so that they could extend
their honeymoon by joining the family's annual exodus
to the beach for the duration of the long hot summer.

Orchestrating the transportation of everybody and everything
they needed was a production almost as grand as a wedding
and not to be missed for anything. Two carriages were added
to the end of the local train for the journey from Philadelphia
to the Delaware shore, just to carry family, friends, servants,
trunks of clothes and even their cow so they were never short
of fresh milk. But of course.

The Sleepy Hollow Country Club dance was in full swing when Betty Jackson arrived wearing her daring new evening gown on a balmy summer evening in 1930.

From the front, Betty's silk dress and beaded bodice looked entirely proper but when she turned around it was a whole other story. Following the fashion some leading Hollywood actresses had set in response to a studio directive outlawing plunging necklines at the Oscars, Betty's stylish scooped backline showed rather more flesh than anyone in Sleepy Hollow was used to seeing.

Betty enjoyed her moment in the spotlight until some roguish young rake decided it was a perfect opportunity to put an ice cube down the back of her dress. Horrified, poor Betty then spent the entire evening trying to stop other mischievious young men following his example.

Having grown up in the west as a beloved daughter of a family descended from pioneers, Martha Rogerson Estabrook loved the social whirl of her new home in Boston when she and her husband moved there after they were married.

Martha especially loved buying clothes for every occasion, and whenever she and her husband were dressed to go out, she would say: 'I think we look really spiffy'.

On this occasion she chose a cranberry silk velvet gown with beaded lace sleeves to host her daughter Emmeline's coming out party in 1930. Eminently spiffy.

Doris barely had time to think about what she would wear to her daughter's wedding. There were caterers to brief, flowers to arrange, seating plans to puzzle over and nerves to soothe.

One day, in between errands, she bought an understated navy silk dress and the deed was done. 'A nice store and a nice dress,' she told her friend Carol, who was horrified: 'Oh, Doris, nice will not do for you. It will not do at all. You are much too spectacular for that.'

Carol told her to come over immediately as she had a dress that would be perfect. A confection of cream-coloured lace and pink silk with a calf-length bouffant skirt, it was indeed divine. Spectacular.

Her friend insisted Doris borrow it and return the blue dress to the store. Doris duly obliged and felt like a million dollars at the wedding. In fact, another friend thought Doris looked so spectacular that she offered to buy the dress for her. But Carol had already planned for Doris to keep it.

Doris loved this dress so much that it became her mother-of-the-bride and mother-of-the-groom dress as she wore it to her other two children's weddings.

Elizabeth Walker Harvey married into English nobility and lived in a grand house in Newfoundland. But as her husband William was a diplomat, they travelled extensively. On her first visit to Bermuda, Elizabeth was bewitched by the cerulean waters and pink-sand beaches so she and her husband returned whenever they could.

On one of their frequent trips 'home' to England in 1867 the Harveys were invited by the Prince and Princess of Wales to a garden party at Marlborough House, Westminster, to be presented to Queen Victoria. Elizabeth commissioned a court dressmaker to create a gown of the most glorious taffeta. Her inspiration for the colours was said to be the coastline of Bermuda: turquoise for the ocean, and tan with a faint pink sheen, for the coastline.

The party was a pleasant but sedate affair. The Queen, who had lately lost her beloved husband, Prince Albert, to typhoid fever, received her guests in a gown of mourning black, the colour she would wear for the rest of her life. The contrast between her gown and the vibrancy of Elizabeth's dress would not have gone unnoticed. But no doubt it would have been politely overlooked as behaviour one would expect from a flamboyant American.

It is 12 May 1937 and the coronation of Their Majesties King George VI and Queen Elizabeth. Eight thousand people are crowded into Westminster Abbey to witness the glittering pageant: the royal families and nobility of Europe, peers of the realm, heads of state and dignitaries from Britain's far-flung colonies and every corner of the globe, all with barely an inch of space between them.

No one does pomp and ceremony like the British, but one American guest at least feels she can hold her own in a flowing Madeleine Vionnet ivory-coloured gown with two trains, one a seamless part of the dress, the other embellished with milky glass beads in the shape of teardrops. In her tiara and headpiece with three ostrich plumes, Lucia feels like royalty herself walking down the aisle to her seat, her silk train curving elegantly behind on the red carpet. After the ceremony, she will remove this second train, as the strict dress code requires.

Suddenly, George VI and his wife, Elizabeth, in elaborate robes of satin, velvet and minerva, enter the abbey, the roar of the throng lining the streets of London following them inside, and Lucia rises with thousands of others to share an historic moment.

Having grown up with a father who was a diplomat, Elissa had travelled the world from an early age and seen things and met people her classmates at college could only dream about.

The experience gave her itchy feet and she became restless staying in any one place for too long. Determined to live independently, ready to take off at a moment's notice, in the 1960s she finally met a kindred spirit in Hans, a sailor and photographer from Denmark.

It was a marriage of minds and opportunity. When Hans married Elissa, he was accepted into the New York Yacht Club, a useful connection for a man who owned a 54-foot schooner where he liked to entertain clients and friends.

For her part, Elissa was delighted to have the means to sail away whenever the mood took her. Like Hans, she loved to throw a party too, spoiling their guests with her culinary skills and showing off her svelte figure in the latest fashions, like this boldly patterned hot-pink mini dress.

When I was eight, my sister and I were sent to stay with Aunt Veronica in her grand Georgian townhouse in Edinburgh. It was exciting but daunting for little girls to be eating in a formal dining room with huge paintings of ancestors staring down, looking like they were waiting for us to use the wrong silverware. After every meal Aunt Veronica would ring the bell for the butler to clear the table.

It was all very *Upstairs, Downstairs* but we loved staying there and especially enjoyed our trips to some of the best toy shops or walking her two cheeky spaniels in the rose gardens in front of her house. Sometimes she bundled us and the dogs into her chauffeured car for walks in the countryside. I remember that whenever I hugged her, I caught the lovely scent of her violet talcum powder.

Seeing her 1930s blue silk jersey dress always brings back those wonderful childhood memories.

Ellen and her fiancé had been planning a spring wedding in 1941 until the day he arrived at her house, ashen-faced, to announce he had been called up following the bombing of Pearl Harbor. He was leaving Boston for the Pacific in three days.

There was no doubt in their minds that they should marry straight away. In special cases like this all the arrangements could be made in a day or two. And that's how Ellen found herself in Filene's Basement, nervously shifting through wedding gowns one by one on a metal rack advertising '$16 wedding dresses', along with several other jittery brides-to-be and their mothers.

Ellen paused as she came to a deceptively simple ivory dress with a slight sheen, cool to the touch. Parachute silk, the label on the dress said. Somehow this seemed right to her. Perhaps a dress made of this would provide her and her fiancé with a safe landing in such dangerous times.

The dress turned out to be such a good luck charm that two of her friends wore it for their wartime weddings.

Delia Marshall was the most popular girl in Doris's class for all the usual reasons - she was beautiful, clever and charming - but one other besides. Delia was the genuine article. As Doris put it: 'She was so enchanting that no one was ever jealous of her because Delia was Delia … She was just special and made everyone she spoke to feel special too'.

It would be difficult not to be a little bit envious of this knockout 1950s gown with its intricate beaded bodice and flowing mushroom chiffon skirt.

Delia always had plenty of men waiting on the sidelines wanting to ask her to dance. And she loved to dance. No one who saw the dreamy faraway look on Delia's face as she twirled in her partner's arms could doubt it.

C louds of blue chiffon float from a jewelled bodice so perfectly fitted that it's almost sinful.

It was love at first sight when Jennifer Johnson saw this magical gown in the window of '220', an exclusive boutique in Sydney's upmarket Double Bay, also known as 'Double Pay', in 1950. But it was worth every penny.

Together they made every other woman green with envy at the Picnic Races Ball in Armidale.

This 1940s chocolate brown crepe dress with beaded flowers belonged to my American grandmother, Granny Smith, who was very formal and always insisted on dining in a grand manner.

Granny would dress for dinner and insist on everyone else in the family following suit. She always wore short white gloves and they stayed on throughout the meal. My father and his brothers had to wear white gloves for dinner too. There was no gnawing on corn cobs or chewing on a bone for them.

I loved my granny but she was, as they say, formidable.

Inspired by Princess Grace's wedding dress, this beautiful lace 1950s gown belonged to the first girl in her family - and her street - to have a wedding dress made out of material that wasn't a hand-me-down.

When Amy's older sister became engaged during the Second World War it was almost impossible to find material suitable for a wedding dress. But luckily her grandmother was a shameless hoarder as well as a champion seamstress. After rummaging around in an old trunk in the attic she emerged, triumphantly clutching a peerless piece of white damask she'd been keeping just in case. From this, she created a small miracle of a dress in the latest style, even managing to add a modest train.

Soon after the wedding, a neighbour asked if she could borrow the dress for her daughter's wedding day. Then another and another. Soon it seemed like half the street wore that dress over the next few years.

But when it came to Amy's turn, the women of the family decreed that the 'something new' had to be her dress, and she owed it to the neighbourhood to make it the most beautiful wedding dress they had ever seen.

The tag inside this tulle and diamante ballgown reads 'De Pinna, 5th Ave, NYC', a designer renowned for creating glamorous masterpieces.

So 20-year-old Kay must have thought all her Christmases had come at once when she received this precious gift from her aunt in New York, just in time to show it off at the 1956 National Catholic Girls Movement Ball in Brisbane.

The ball was held at the grand Cloudland Dance Hall, the place to meet someone in those days. With its huge polished dance floor, glittering chandeliers and domed skylights, Cloudland looked like a movie set. An upper circle of tiered seating offered a spectacular view of all the action on the dance floor, and velvet curtains cordoned off private alcoves for those who'd prefer to avoid the limelight.

But there would have been no suggestion of such hijinks for Kay. After all, her date was 'organised' by a priest.

E cru organdie trimmed with black lace, this elegant gown was one of the more understated choices of a woman who loved dramatic clothes. According to Doris, Audrey Chancellor came to every party at their house dressed so spectacularly that everyone would applaud.

Audrey had a secret source - the annual second-hand clothing sale in aid of the Episcopal Church in Philadelphia. Most of the clothes were donated by the grand dames of the city and the pickings were rich.

When Doris showcased her collection at Bryn Mawr College, Audrey had the idea of seeing if she could contribute something from a special beneficiary. Her first husband's partner was a close friend of screen legend Katharine Hepburn, and Audrey decided that something of hers would be a coup for Doris.

Doris thought no more about it until she got a phone call one day from none other than Katharine Hepburn. Katharine said she wished she could send something, but unfortunately her collection of clothing had been promised to a dear friend. Typically, Doris just thought it was fun to talk to her on the telephone.

This spectacular 1880s striped silk Victorian bustle gown was a treasured vintage piece owned by another passionate collector I'm sure Doris would have loved to meet.

Deborah McKeown was also a gifted seamstress so she recreated many of the six hundred dresses she collected and wore them to the Victorian Society's gatherings in Adelaide. Like Doris, she was fastidious about accessorising her outfits and wearing her hair in the period style.

Doris would be delighted to know that her collection has been enriched by pieces collected by a kindred spirit.

Acknowledgements

Dreaming of Dior has been a truly collaborative book and everyone has been instrumental in creating it - and getting it to the printers on time! My special thanks go to:

Grant Cowan, whose incredible skill as an artist transformed each treasured dress into a to-die-for illustration. It was so much fun working on this together.

To the wonderful dynamic team at HarperCollins Australia, Consulting Publisher Fiona Henderson and Senior Editor Jo Butler for their unwavering belief and commitment that this was 'the little book that could', and for their positive guidance and editing.

To Creative Director Helen Biles for seeing the big picture, along with editor Kim Swivel. Thanks also to Annabel Blay, Natalie Costa Bir, Marie Slocombe, Jane Waterhouse and everyone working behind the scenes at HarperCollins. Their expertise, guidance and enthusiasm has been phenomenal.

To Penelope Leonard and Katrina Skinner, my supportive friends and colleagues at ESMOD Australia.

My beautiful daughter Olivia, who patiently sat through countless long meetings.

My parents, Noble and Margaret, who gave me the confidence to go out and enjoy life at its fullest. And, of course, all the wonderful donors who gave their treasures and stories to Doris and me 'in love and in trust'.